"Ty and Daneen Bottler are no ___
and prophetic voices to the b ___
dearest friends. I have watched them as a couple and individually live out the words that they speak, teach, and write. They strive with great intentionality to 'become like Christ' in all that they do — before God and before men. The words in this devotional have been forged in the crucible of their own lives; therefore they are written out of the authority and anointing that accompanies living in the pure convictions that they hold dear. They are not satisfied with the status quo of mere Christianity but reach to become more like Christ with every passing day. This devotional will stir hunger within you, and it will begin a deeper work of transformation in your heart and life. If you long to become like Jesus — this devotional will serve as a threshold to fill the deepest longings of your heart."

KATHI PELTON Author *Finding Home: a Doorway of Hope,* Co-founder Inscribe Ministries

"It has been my privilege to know Ty and Daneen Bottler for more than a decade. These two are the real deal! They are courageous, consistent, servant-hearted 'equippers' who live their lives with burning hearts and a deep love for the Lord and His church. It would seem from my perspective, that their greatest desire is to truly know God... and to help others know Him too.

"Ty and Daneen love the church and live with a deep longing, even restlessness, for the people of God to walk in the fullness of the New covenant.

"This desire to 'equip the saints' is clearly displayed in their new book *BECOMING.* While being an inspiration work, this book is far more than that. It contains clearly articulated tools that will help every reader to dive deeper into the Truth, and live worthy of the One who has called them. I thoroughly recommend this book and its authors."

KRISTEN WILLIAMS Pastor, Prophetic Minister, and Revivalist

"I have known Ty and Daneen Bottler for years. In that time, I have noticed two consistent themes in their lives. Those two themes are a passion for God and a passion for people to know God at a deeper level. Those dual passions fill the pages of this book. As you read through *BECOMING* you will feel the hand of God reach out and touch your heart. That is why the Bottlers wrote this book."
GARRIS ELKINS Author, Mentor, and Prophetic Minister

"*BECOMING* provides a broad and powerful set of tools to help you identify areas in need of upgrade and to activate you into a richer, deeper and more impactful walk with God."
JEREMY HAUG Business owner and Advisor

BECOMING

Ty & Daneen Bottler

BEC
OM
ING

A 30 DAY JOURNEY
TO PERSONAL TRANSFORMATION

Inscribe Press
Creativity Unleashed

Published 2022 by Inscribe Press, Hillsboro, OR 97124.
Printed in the United States of America.
Cover design by Sarah Haug.

ISBN 978-1-951611-31-6 (paperback)
978-1-951611-32-3 (eBook)

CONTENTS

INTRODUCTION

How it started

ERE THEY WERE, THE THREE closest disciples of Jesus, standing on top of a mountain with the Master, and right before their eyes He was transformed into something different. It had only been about a week earlier that Jesus started talking about His death and that He was going to come back in His Father's glory, but still — whatever Jesus had already told them, they had no idea what He meant until they stood gazing at what He had become. Then, both Moses and Elijah showed up and started talking to Jesus. As if the sight of the bright, shining face of the Son of God, and His white-as-light clothes weren't enough to bring the fear of God into the disciples, the appearance of these two historical figures, both of whom had not seen the face of the earth for almost a thousand years, would have. On top of that, Father God came in a cloud and began speaking to them all, affirming His Son. Imagine the three disciples looking around at each other and wondering why any of them were invited to this party. In the presence of such holiness and glory, the Bible records them falling on their faces in a state of terror. Eventually they looked up, and all that was left to see was Jesus in His original state.

At the end of this story, we read that Jesus instructed Peter, James, and John not to tell anyone what had happened on that mountain until He had risen from the dead. You can imagine how much these three disciples would have loved to tell the others about the encounter, because you better believe that they knew the significance of what had just happened. This important story eventually got out; in fact, three of the four gospels directly record what happened, and some say the fourth (John's) alludes to it in the fourteenth verse of the first chapter, when it says "The Word became flesh and made his dwelling among us.

We have seen his glory, the glory of the one and only Son, who came from the Father, full of grace and truth."

Regardless of whether John was specifically talking about this particular occasion, the idea of earthly bodies becoming transfigured was a concept that was carried on through the writings of our earliest church fathers. Besides its use to describe the transfiguration of Jesus, the Greek word, metamorphoo was used two other times in the New Testament. In Paul's letter to the Romans, he encourages the church to become transformed by the renewing of their minds. Also, in 2 Corinthians 3, Paul states that we are being transformed into God's image with ever-increasing glory. Why would Paul use the same word to describe what God's people are becoming as was used to describe the transformation of Jesus? Perhaps Jesus's transfiguration was a foreshadowing of what God is calling all of His children to become.

We know what you're probably thinking. How can we become as bright and shiny as what Jesus looked like? Many Christians have a hard enough time just keeping the faith, let alone getting to the point of shining with God's glory. Fear and shame have kept a lid on so many in the church, and lack of faith has led to this idea of us becoming transfigured appearing as foreign a concept as us growing gills and breathing under water! And yet, regardless of the unbelief of so many, this is still what God intends for us to look like. Jesus becoming transfigured while He was still alive, and Paul's invitation to all believers to become transformed, is our permission to explore what transfiguration means, and how that transformation is manifested in our lives.

What's the point?

We want to make sure that that you understand that personal transformation is not the point of this book. A greater walk with the Lord, and Him having a greater influence on your actions and thoughts, is the goal. Whether it's through this book or other means, transformation will be a fruit of your surrender to the Lord and His work in your life.

Unfortunately, many in the church have gotten their focus on God hijacked. We believe that there's a legitimate desire in people to draw closer to God, but all too often, many get sidetracked from acting upon that desire. There are a number of reasons for this to happen, but two of the biggest ways are for people getting wrapped up in the affairs of their lives, and only giving a small portion of their thoughts and time to their walk with God. Another way, which is on the opposite side of the spectrum from the first reason mentioned, is people pursuing spiritual experiences, rather than pursuing God. There's a type of culture that appeals to those who go from one conference to another, seeking the latest and greatest spiritual manifestation. This is not to say that there aren't hungry people with good intentions going to conferences. However, sometimes what is being sought can get skewed, and people can very easily begin to focus on manifestations, which can lead to a cycle of perpetually going from event to event, trying to get their spiritual "fix." This type of life will never be fulfilling because we were designed to pursue God, not spiritual experiences. When we prioritize spiritual experience above relationship with God, we end up fooling ourselves into thinking that we are being led by God, when in actuality, we are being led by manifestation. If we follow manifestations, we're going to get manifestations. But one of the many dangers of focusing on them rather than Jesus, is that what is manifested stands a good chance of having its origins in something other than God. Transformation or transfiguration is not the goal, and it's not even the point of our walk with God. Knowing Jesus and bringing Him glory is the purpose of our lives, and if our hearts are set on this goal, then we can be confident that what is manifested through us will be good.

Personal transformation is the fruit of a life lived for the glory of God. In both Romans 12 and 2 Corinthians 3, Paul speaks of two things, worship and beholding God, that result in transformation. We must recognize that in both of these, the focus is squarely on God, not on ourselves; as stated earlier, the goal is the pursuit of Jesus, and not the pursuit of manifestations. Romans twelve starts off encouraging us to offer our bodies as living sacrifices to God as a demonstration of our true worship to Him. It then goes on to instruct us not to conform to the patterns of the world, but become transformed by the renewing of our minds. There are two things about these verses that stick out. The first is that Paul tells us that the end result of this process is transformation, to the point that we are able to test and approve God's will. But Paul also says that this process happens while we are living, so because of this, we can be sure that transformation is not just reserved for when we die and receive new bodies, but it is for the here and now. The second thing that sticks out about this verse is that this process is initiated by our worship to God. Once again, God is the focus, not transformation. When we properly align our lives to the purposes of God and we keep Him as the focus, we can be sure that glorious things will happen to us.

There was a season where the children of Israel were in the desert, and Moses was consistently in the presence of God. God would call Moses into the tent of meeting to speak and commune with Him. The result of these encounters left the face of Moses shining, so he covered his face with a veil when he spoke to the Israelites. In 2 Corinthians 3, Paul talks about this story of Moses, and he makes the point that, as bright as the face of Moses was, it was nothing in comparison to the glory that awaits those who are in the new covenant. Once again, transformation is not the point in this passage either, because Paul says in verse 18 that beholding the glory of the Lord produces the fruit of transformation. Beholding the presence of God is the goal, and the result of that encounter is a spiritual and a physical manifestation of His glory. Living in the presence of God will result in His glory being displayed through our lives.

Ultimately, our lives were meant to be lived in a state of worship and intimacy with God. All the other things in this life will line up in proper order if we get those first two right. Relationships, provision, ministry, transformation, and many other good things will be the fruit of living a life that is focused on worshipping God and living in His presence.

Give it 30 days

Will this book guarantee that you will become transformed in thirty days? No, of course not. Can it be a tool to help you become transformed in thirty days? Yes, most definitely! This book is not meant to explore every topic there is in our walk with Christ, but it is meant to be a way for you to engage with God in a greater way. It's also a good way to see where you are properly aligned to His Word, and where you're falling short. Through this book, our biggest hope is that you encounter the presence of Jesus in all the words you read, because we know that, for every one of us, the presence of God is where we become more like Him, and we become transformed.

We've taken thirty different topics that deal with our walk with God, and we've made each topic the focus for each day. Those topics range from identity to the fire of the Holy Spirit, and everything in between. The topics are not intended to be comprehensive, but each one lays a good groundwork for the reader to explore more deeply into the subject if they so desire. Towards the end of each day's reading, there are questions to ask both yourself and the Holy Spirit, to get you to think about where you're at in this process. The final thing to do each day is to pray the written guided prayer. This prayer is most effective if you understand what you are praying and it is spoken in agreement and faith. We encourage you to dive into everything this book has to offer, including asking all the guiding questions, journaling as you go, and fully engaging in the process with faith. Whether this is your first time going through this book, or you've made it an exercise to go through every year, it's a great way to gauge your growth in the things of God.

We pray a blessing on you as you take the next thirty days to draw closer to the heart of God, and courageously take the transformational journey with Him into becoming all that He has intended for you to become.

"Beloved, we are God's children now, and what we will be has not yet appeared; but we know that when he appears we shall be like him, because we shall see him as he is."
The Apostle John

Day 1

HUNGERING AFTER GOD

When you said, "Seek My Face," my heart said to You, "Your face, O Lord, I shall seek." (Psalm 27:8, NASB)

*C*AN YOU RECALL A TIME where you were extremely hungry, and one of your favorite meals was waiting for you, but you still had a couple of hours to wait before you could eat it? Or perhaps you can remember how you felt during a time when you hadn't seen your spouse or loved ones for a long period of time, and you were counting the days when you'd be reunited. There's something about hungering after something that makes it nearly impossible to not have that thing constantly at the forefront of our minds. Whether it's a food you really like, or a person that has captured your attention, when you desire to have that object of affection, it's just about the only thing you think about, and you are kept in a constant state of keeping an eye on that thing so that you don't miss an opportunity for interaction. I know that we've all, at one point or another, experienced these feelings for a person or an object, but when can we honestly say was the last time that we've felt that for God?

There's something about hunger that captures our attention. This is why it's so important to make sure that we find ourselves in a constant state of desiring more of God. Having a hunger, and being satisfied is one of the tensions that followers of Christ get to navigate. When we say yes to His invitation for more of Him, a hunger for Him grows, and He comes and satisfies. But then we hunger for more of God, and once again He comes and satisfies. The reason that this cycle can go on for eternity, is that our God is eternal, and it will take eternity to fully grasp His love and goodness. Unfortunately, many eventually take their eyes off of God, and begin focusing on themselves or other things, and they get off of the hunger train. One of the things about this train, is that the longer amount of time that you've been off of it, the harder it is to remember how significant it was when you were on it. This is why people can stray so far away from an intimate walk with God, and not even realize how far they've gone. But, praise God that regardless of where we find ourselves, or how long it's been since we've gotten on the tracks of hungering after God, that train is waiting for us to get back on, and there's a ticket with our name on it, just sitting there for us to grab. Our hunger after God will assure us that He is getting our full attention, and when He has our attention, we can be confident that He will lead us and guide us into all that He has for us in this amazing journey of life.

Meditate on Psalm 27:8. Say it out loud a few times. Really think about how it applies to you. Ask yourself:

- Do I even know that God has invited me to know Him more?
- Do I even have a desire for deeper intimacy with God?

Ask the Holy Spirit:

- "Do I hear Your invitation for intimacy?"
- "Do I hunger for more of You?"
- "Are there times that I let my hunger for You subside?"

Write in your journal what you hear Him say.

Day 1 DEVOTIONAL PRAYER

"God, I thank You for Your invitation into a deeper place in You. Thank You that You desire to be intimate with me, and that You want to walk and talk with me every hour of every day. I can only have a hunger for You because You have first demonstrated a hunger for me, so today, I choose to pursue You again. Forgive me for letting my hunger fade and taking my eyes off of you, which has caused me to be focused on other things. I commit myself to always be found in a place of desiring more of You, and to walk in intimacy with You."

Declaration: I am becoming one who maintains my hunger after God, and seeks His face in all I do.

"Accepting the Cross, entering into fellowship with Christ, means entering the realm of transformation."
Pope Benedict XVI

Day 2

REPENTANCE

"If my people who are called by my name humble themselves,
and pray and seek my face and turn from their wicked ways,
then I will hear from heaven and will forgive their sin and heal
their land." (2 Chronicles 7:14, ESV)

FOR MANY OF US, SAYING "I'm sorry" can be a hard thing to do. No one likes to admit that they were wrong, so when we're faced with owning a mistake, uttering those words can be one of the most challenging things in the world. And if we're truly repentant, admitting to being wrong is more than saying some words; it's the start of changing those issues in our lives that need redeeming.

Despite the difficult nature of repentance, it is a beautiful thing. It's not something that only the worst of sinners should do. It's not a shameful thing that should embarrass us. It's not just a one-time thing we do when we receive Christ. No, repentance is something that should be an active part of every believer's life. Simply put, repentance is acknowledging our shortcomings, receiving the forgiveness of our sins — which God has already released — and recommitting ourselves to walk in His grace, so the fruit of our lives produces more righteousness. This is not to make light of our shortcomings, because, as Charles Spurgeon said, "There is no repentance where a man can talk lightly of sin, much less where he can speak tenderly and lovingly of it." However, there is a balance of acknowledging sin in our lives, but not allowing those shortcomings to weigh us down to the point we feel paralyzed. Paul said in Romans 3 that "all have sinned and fallen short of the glory of God," but through God's grace and mercy, and through repentance, He has made a way for realignment in our lives so we may continue walking as His sons and daughters. If we lay down the pride and rebellion that we have agreed with, and repent of our wrong actions and mindsets, we can walk in the mind of Christ and become a catalyst for healing and restoration to the people and the land around us.

Meditate on 2 Chronicles 7:14. Say it out loud a few times. Really think about how it applies to you. Ask yourself:

- What does it mean to seek God's face and turn from wickedness?
- What does the healing of my land (family, possessions, relationships) look like?

Ask the Holy Spirit:

- "Is there anything in me that needs Your redeeming touch?"
- "Are there any agreements with the enemy that I've allowed?"
- "Are there places in my life that I don't have the faith to believe for transformation?"

Write in your journal what you hear Him say.

Day 2 DEVOTIONAL PRAYER

"God, I confess that I have fallen short of your glory. I've made agreements with fear and doubt, and I've chosen my own way. Forgive me for my mindsets that have not aligned with yours. Forgive me for acting out of my dysfunction, instead of relying on your grace and strength. I commit myself to setting my eyes on You and looking to You for wisdom. Thank you that your grace is sufficient, and is new every morning. So, in the name of Jesus, I break off every agreement with the enemy, and with the grace and faith that You have released, I will see victories in every area of my life and receive healing and restoration of the land that the enemy has stolen."

<u>Declaration</u>: I am becoming one who walks in a lifestyle of repentance as an important key to my growth in Christ.

Journal

"Keeping the gospel in focus, you see, is more than helping our children know forgiveness of sin through repentance and faith in Jesus Christ. In the gospel there is the promise of internal transformation and empowerment."
Tedd Tripp

FORGIVENESS

"And whenever you stand praying, forgive, if you have anything against anyone, so that your Father also who is in heaven may forgive you your trespasses." (Mark 11:25, ESV)

OVER THE YEARS, WE'VE HAD the opportunity to come alongside many people and help them in their journey of being led by the Lord and growing closer to Him. In those times when individuals have found themselves feeling "stuck," or not able to discern the Lord's direction, we asked them if there were any places of unforgiveness in their heart. Almost always, there were people who had hurt them, and they were holding on to the pain caused by those wounds. We've discovered that one of the main ways people keep themselves from progressing in their walk with the Lord is by nurturing unforgiveness.

Forgiveness is an important doorway to healing, and it positions us to hear and receive from God. We live in a fallen world with broken people. Because of this, we've all been hurt by others, just as we've hurt other people. Holding onto the wrongs done to us not only keeps wounds from healing, it empowers the perpetrator's actions to keep victimizing us long after the initial offense. There's something inside us that longs for justice, and when justice seems like it's not happening in our circumstances, we often feel our only option is to hold on to offense. Unfortunately, this leads to a cycle of constant wounding and pain, instead of healing. Romans 12:19 says, "Vengeance is mine, I will repay, says the Lord." So, even if the offender never asks for forgiveness, we need to be able to place our hurts and wounds at the loving feet of Jesus, knowing that His justice and righteousness will prevail. Besides the healing that comes with forgiving sins, it's also a part of the commission that Jesus gave His followers. Once forgiveness is released, a pathway for healing and wholeness is created, which will give everyone involved a greater capacity to be led by the Holy Spirit.

Meditate on Mark 11:25. Say it out loud a few times. Really think about how it applies to you. Ask yourself:

- What does it mean to truly release forgiveness to someone?

- How hypocritical is it to expect God to forgive me, when I don't forgive others?

Ask the Holy Spirit:

- "Is the blockage I feel from receiving from You a result of me holding onto unforgiveness?"

- "What wounds am I holding onto that I need to give to You?"

- "Do I believe that You will be my vindicator?"

Write in your journal what you hear Him say.

Day 3 DEVOTIONAL PRAYER

"God, I thank You for dying for me. Thank You that Your blood has washed me clean and freed me of all my guilt. Please forgive me for not forgiving others who have hurt me. Forgive me for holding on to my pain and making it part of my identity. Give me the courage to release forgiveness to all the people who have harmed me, and even though some of them have never apologized, I choose to give those situations into Your righteous hands. I exchange my hurts for Your healing, and my rejection for Your acceptance. In this divine exchange, wash over the wounds that have kept me focused on my pain and bound by unforgiveness, and free me from the prison that I have chosen to live in. Let my mind and thoughts be opened to receive from You, and let me walk in confidence, knowing that You are my defender and the lifter of my head."

Declaration: I am becoming one who is quick to forgive, and quick to receive forgiveness, as well as one who is not easily offended.

Journal

_____

_____

_____

_____

_____

_____

_____

_____

_____

_____

_____

_____

_____

"The faith in Christ that saves us from our sins involves an internal transformation that has external implications."
David Platt

Day 4

THE FEAR OF THE LORD

Let us hear the conclusion of the whole matter; fear God and
keep His commandments, for this is man's all.
(Ecclesiastes 12:13, NKJV)

I f there's one thing that we've discovered in this last season, it's the
awareness of how much fear drives people. Politicians, businesses,
and the demonic have weaponized fear to manipulate and cause
people to walk away from who they are truly called to be. But
unlike the type of fear that the enemy uses, the fear of the Lord
does not make you afraid of God; the fear of the Lord causes you to
run to God, not away from him. Having the fear of the Lord means
we are actively giving God the glory, honor, reverence, thanksgiving,
praise, and preeminence He deserves. We not only believe in God, but
we obey Him. When we put something else in the place of lordship in
our lives, we are making it an idol and serving it.

The reality is that whatever we fear, we will serve. If we do not fear
the Lord, we will end up fearing man. If you fear God, you will serve
Him. If you fear man, you will serve man. You must choose. Fearing
the Lord causes us to live by God's ways and standards, not our own; it
means that we have surrendered our lives to Him fully, acknowledging
Christ Jesus as Lord and King over everything. The fear of the Lord
is clean and pure, and it moves us into righteousness through His
loving-kindness. This causes us to want to be near God and in His
presence. Our perspectives become aligned correctly when we look at
Christ Jesus and see Him as He is: supreme, majestic, all-powerful, the
Author and Finisher of our faith. Circumstances, opposition, emotional states become small compared to the greatness and surpassing glory
of Christ Jesus. It is only by living in this attitude of holy fear that we
can flourish and enter the wisdom and blessings of Christ.

Here are a few blessings promised to those who fear the Lord:
Answers (Heb 5:7), God's abounding goodness (Psalm 31:19),

Angelic protection (Ps 34:7), God's attention (Ps 33:18), Provision (Ps 34:9), God's great mercy (Ps 103:11), Wisdom and understanding (Pro 9:10-11), Peace of mind (Pro 15:6), Clarity and direction (Ps 25:12).

Meditate on Ecclesiastes 12:13. Say it out loud a few times. Really think about how it applies to you. Ask yourself:

- Have I become so familiar with information about God that I've become irreverent toward Him?
- How is obedience linked to fearing the Lord?

Ask the Holy Spirit:

- "Is there anything that I have placed in the lordship position of my life over You?"
- "What areas in my life do I still need to surrender to You?"
- "Show me the places where I have been afraid of You, instead of running to You and Your perfect love."

Write in your journal what you hear Him say.

Day 4 DEVOTIONAL PRAYER

"Father in Heaven, in the name of Jesus, I humble myself and come to You to seek Your mercy and grace. I long to love, fear and know You. I ask forgiveness for any disrespect or hypocrisy towards You that I have tolerated in my life. I turn to you Jesus, as my Savior and Lord. You are my Master and I give my life completely to You. Fill me with Your love and holy fear. I desire to know You intimately in a deeper dimension than I have ever known anyone or anything else. I acknowledge my dependency on the Holy Spirit and ask that You would fill me now. Thank you for the abundant mercy and grace You have poured out upon me, and for all that You have done and are about to do, I give You glory and praise."

Declaration: I am becoming one who recognizes the supremacy and majesty of God, and I place Him in the highest place of influence in my life.

Journal

"The speculative thinker makes Christianity into theology, instead of recognizing that a living relationship to Christ involves passion, struggle, decision, personal appropriation, and inner transformation."
Charles E. Moor

Day 5

RIGHTEOUSNESS

He made Christ who knew no sin to [judicially] be sin on our behalf, so that in Him we would become the righteousness of God [that is, we would be made acceptable to Him and placed in a right relationship with Him by His gracious lovingkindness].
(2 Corinthians 5:21, AMP)

*H*AVE YOU EVER HAD ONE of those days, weeks, or seasons where everything in the world just felt right? Obviously, we all go through difficulties in life, whether it be financial setbacks, broken relationships, deaths, or physical ailments, but sometimes we can get a brief reprieve from those challenges. And it's then that we feel on top of the world. Believe it or not, we can have this same feeling about our walk with God, because He has called us His righteousness. Righteousness is simply defined as being in right standing or right relationship with God. Jesus paid the ultimate price, His very life, for us to be reconciled to the Father. His blood atoned for our sin and brought us into right relationship with Him. There is nothing in ourselves that can produce righteousness, but it is only in Christ Jesus that we are made righteous. It is the lovingkindness of God that leads us to repentance, and as we encounter God's great love, the desire for right relationship with Him is birthed.

We cannot earn our righteousness. It only comes through faith in Christ Jesus. Not only does the blood of Jesus bring us into right relationship with God, but when we take Him at His word and obey His voice, righteousness is made manifest to the world. Romans 4 says that Abraham believed God and it was credited to him as righteousness, but it was Abraham's obedience to the voice of God that demonstrated his faith. Just like Abraham, every step of faith in Christ that we take produces a harvest of righteousness in our hearts. If we truly believe God's Word, and in faith receive the truth that Christ has made us

31

righteous, then we will live a life unto the Lord. This type of life that obeys God's Word and has full confidence in who He is, will produce the fruit of righteousness.

Meditate on 2 Corinthians 5:21. Say it out loud a few times. Really think about how it applies to you. Ask yourself:

- What does it mean to be righteous?
- What qualifies me as righteous?

Ask the Holy Spirit:

- "Is there any shame in my life keeping me from accepting the truth that You are my righteousness?"
- "Am I still trying to become righteousness in my own strength?"
- "Is my life producing the fruit of righteousness?"

Write in your journal what you hear Him say.

Day 5 DEVOTIONAL PRAYER

"Lord Jesus, thank you for giving Your life so that I could be reconciled to the Father. Thank you that by your precious blood being shed on the cross, you have made me righteous. Holy Spirit, I ask that You produce in me a hunger for Your righteousness. Let your love lead me on the paths of righteousness for Your name's sake; that through my life, the world would see and know You. I thank You for making me righteous and giving me the grace to obey You and to walk in your ways, the grace to step out in faith, knowing that You are my sufficiency."

Declaration: I am becoming the righteousness of God and I walk with confidence, knowing that I am in right standing with Him.

Journal

"The needed transformation is very largely a matter of replacing in ourselves those idea systems of evil (and their corresponding cultures) with the idea system that Jesus Christ embodied and taught and with a culture of the kingdom of God."
Dallas Willard

Day 6

WORSHIP

"But the hour is coming, and is now here, when the true
worshipers will worship the Father in spirit and truth, for the
Father is seeking such people to worship him."
(John 4:23, ESV)

IT'S INTERESTING TO SEE HOW much time, money, and attention the world gives to celebrities, movie stars, and athletes. The world is fascinated with people of higher status than them, and our culture worships celebrity. Oh sure, the average person would never admit to worshipping their favorite actor or actress, but the amount of attention given to famous people speaks volumes as to where people are spending their focus and affection. Is it no wonder that this culture has leaked into many parts of the church, where celebrity preachers and musicians take a lot of the attention for themselves, and away from God? But this type of worship will always leave the worshipper hollow and longing for something different, because we were made to live a life of worship unto God.

Just as we are taking these thirty days to seek the Lord in a greater way, God is seeking for a people who will live a life of worshipping Him in spirit and in truth. He is looking for a people who don't rely on a time or place to dedicate to Him, but who give Him every minute of every day,. Worship is not just a time of singing songs. Yes, singing together is a wonderful expression of worship, but so often we lose sight of the importance of our everyday life as an act of worship to Him. In Colossians 3, we are instructed to do all things as unto the Lord. This means that we should offer every part of our lives as an act of worship to God. If we're at home, or work, or school, or at the coffee shop — regardless of what we're doing — every action should be done with a mindset of glorifying God.

Acts 17 says that "...in Him we live and we move and we have our being." So, invite the presence of God into your day. Do your work with God in mind. Enjoy hanging out with your friends, but honor the Lord in your conversations. Raise your children to love the presence of God and demonstrate your relationship with Him as a natural part of life, not just something you do on Sundays. These are the actions of the type of people that God is seeking after.

Meditate on John 4:23. Say it out loud a few times. Really think about how it applies to you. Ask yourself:

- Have I given my worship to other people or things?
- Do my actions at work and home demonstrate a life of worship?

Ask the Holy Spirit:

- "Have I truly given You every part of my day?"
- "Do I view everything I do as an act of worship to You?"
- "What does it mean to worship in spirit and in truth?"

Write in your journal what you hear Him say.

Day 6 DEVOTIONAL PRAYER

"God, I respond to your call of living a life of worship. Forgive me for holding back parts of my life for my own, and not submitting them to You. Forgive me for not dedicating every aspect of my life as a sacrifice of praise to You. Today, I choose to worship You in spirit and in truth. I invite You into every minute of my day and welcome Your influence into all of my decisions. Let my actions at home and work, and every other place life finds me, bring glory to Your name. I will enjoy being with my friends, conduct my conversations with honor, diligently work at my employment, and lovingly raise my children with the same passion and mindset that I have when I'm praying and singing songs of worship to You. I love You, Lord, and I love to worship You. So, let the words of my mouth, the actions of my life, and the meditations of my heart be acceptable in Your sight."

<u>Declaration</u>: I am becoming one who worships God in everything I do, and brings Him glory through my words and actions.

Journal

"The Bible was written not to satisfy your curiosity but to help you conform to Christ's image. Not to make you a smarter sinner but to make you like the Saviour. Not to fill your head with a collection of biblical facts but to transform your life."
Howard G. Hendricks

Day 7

CONSECRATING OUR MINDSETS

Don't copy the behavior and customs of this world, but let God transform you into a new person by changing the way you think. Then you will learn to know God's will for you, which is good and pleasing and perfect. (Romans 12:2, NLT)

THE GREATEST BATTLES ON THIS earth will not take place in some remote land, being waged by vast armies, but they will be found in the minds of every living person. There is a continual war being waged to gain influence over how people think and make decisions, and the first key to winning this war is to recognize that we are actually in one! In Ephesians 6, Paul encourages us to put on the whole armor of God to help us resist the strategies of the enemy. The word "strategy" as used in this Scripture means cunning arts, deceit, trickery; and the word has a sense of movement to it. The enemy is constantly trying to place himself in front of us. He's not engaging us with stagnant temptations, but is attacking us with an on-going, frontal assault to distort and skew our mindsets and worldview. So, it's clear that we must be vigilant in guarding these, and submitting them to Christ. Consecrating our mindsets means that we do not entertain any thoughts that rise up above the lordship of Jesus.

Through circumstances, the enemy will try to tempt us with the following to compromise our mindsets:

1. Believing that our ways are better than God's ways
2. Holding back certain parts of our lives from God
3. Being in a hurry, and not allowing time to process with Holy Spirit
4. Bonding with disappointment and negative experiences
5. Isolating and not allowing wise people to speak into our lives
6. Being led by emotions.

Our mindsets will affect our actions. If our mindsets remain unredeemed, the enemy will trap us into a cycle of destructive decisions and behaviors, but if we recognize the enemy's tactics, and we consecrate and submit our mindsets to Christ, we will come into a fruitful and effective life.

Meditate on Romans 12:2. Say it out loud a few times. Really think about how it applies to you. Ask yourself:

- Am I allowing culture to disciple my mindsets?
- Am I constantly struggling with unbelief or fear?

Ask the Holy Spirit:

- "Am I actively submitting my mindsets to You?
- "Am I allowing You to transform my thinking?"
- "Do I have peace about Your will for my life?"

Write in your journal what you hear Him say.

Day 7 DEVOTIONAL PRAYER

"God, I invite You into every thought in my mind. I submit my thinking into your hands, and I ask that You heal and redeem every place that I've given agreement to the enemy. Forgive me for allowing myself to be discipled by the world. I take back every agreement and thought that has raised itself above Your lordship, and I place it at Your feet. I exchange fear for Your love, worry for Your peace, and death for Your life. Renew my mind every day, so that my life will become transformed, and so that I can live effectively for Your Kingdom, and bring You glory and honor."

Declaration: My mindsets are becoming redeemed as I take every thought captive and submit them to the lordship of Jesus Christ.

Journal

(blank lined journal page with faint background text: "BECOMING" down the left margin and "MINDSETS" down the right margin)

"The Holy Spirit accompanies God's Word to bring revelation of Christ, resulting in transformation."
Bob Hoskins

Day 8

CONSECRATING OUR SOULS

Do not offer any part of yourself to sin as an instrument of wickedness, but rather offer yourselves to God as those who have been brought from death to life; and offer every part of yourself to Him as an instrument of righteousness.
(Romans 6:13, NIV)

IT OFTEN SEEMS THAT PEOPLE who use the term "innocent as a child" have never had children. Also, they probably have never seen the disposition or heard the screams of a child who is not getting their way. There's something inside us that wants our own way, beginning the day we are born. God gave us the gift of free will, but sin has taken its toll on how we exercise that free will. Even though unredeemed man is still hard at work, accomplishing things for himself, and living for the benefit of himself, God has called His children to a different kind of lifestyle – a life of consecration, which is the process of making something holy and devoting it solely for the purposes of God.

The apostle Paul instructs us to offer every part of ourselves to the Lord; this means our whole being (mind, will, emotions, and body). Sometimes we choose to compartmentalize what part of ourselves we give to the Lord; in doing so, we are withholding from Him. Our will and emotions need to be submitted to the Spirit of God just as much as our minds. When we operate from the soul, we control what we want, do what we want, feel what we want, act how we want, and decide when we want things to happen. Essentially, we give in to the trap of becoming our own god, a deceptive tactic the enemy uses to get us to walk down a path that leads to death. While "seizing the wheel" may cause us to feel we have momentary control, the truth is that our sin has control of us. It is only through — and in — Christ Jesus, that we have true life, and life to the fullest. Consecrating our mind, will, and emotions (soul) leads to holiness in Christ; this means that we choose to submit to the lordship of the Holy Spirit, allowing Him to determine how we choose to live, what we choose to believe, and even how we process our emotions and responses. When we consecrate ourselves, we are devoting every thought, action, and choice to serve the purpose and will of God. Giving up control can be a scary proposition, but ultimately it's the only way that we will live our lives to their fullest potential.

Meditate on Romans 6:13. Say it out loud a few times. Really think about how it applies to you. Ask yourself:

- What does it mean to have my life consecrated to the Lord?
- Why is it important to submit not only my mindsets to God, but also my will and emotions?

Ask the Holy Spirit:

- "Are there any areas in my soul (mind, will, emotions) that I have withheld from you?"
- "Am I actively allowing you to lead my thinking, my responses and my actions during the day?"
- "Do I trust you to lead me, or am I scared of the future?"

Write in your journal what you hear Him say.

Day 8 DEVOTIONAL PRAYER

"Father, I set my gaze on You. I choose to place You in the driver's seat of my life. I ask Lord, that by Your blood You would come and cleanse me from all unrighteousness. I yield my will to Your will. I surrender my thoughts to be renewed to Your thoughts. I surrender my heart to be transformed by Your love, so it will reflect Your heart. Thank You, Jesus, for Your blood that not only cleanses me but sets me apart for Your purposes. I willingly invite You to shape me and mold me as You see fit. I trust You and know that Your love for me is unending. Thank You for transforming this jar of clay into a vessel of honor, holy and acceptable for Your purposes – in Jesus's name!"

Declaration: My soul is becoming an instrument of righteousness as I offer every part of my being to the Lord for His use.

"When we share Christ, the Truth behind our transformation, we are offering people an opportunity to be transformed."
David Jeremiah

Day 9

CONSECRATING OUR FAMILIES

"For I have known him, in order that he may command his children and his household after him, that they keep the way of the Lord, to do righteousness and justice"
(Genesis 18:19, NKJV)

OUR FIRST MISSION FIELD IS TO our families. We have known many people full of enthusiasm to reach the world for Christ, but they sacrificed their families to attain something that they thought was a higher call. The truth is, families are the first and greatest call God has given each believer. A culture of honor, which is passed down from generation to generation, causes a ripple effect of extending the Kingdom of God much further than we can see or even realize. God is about family. He's called families to fulfill His purposes on the earth. Even though the above Scripture is talking about Abraham, God has the same intent and goal for each of His children. He wants us to know Him more, so that we can demonstrate His goodness to the generations, and the result is that families follow the Lord and release righteousness and justice on the earth.

Denny Cline, an apostle and author based out of Oregon, recently wrote a book about a word he received from the Lord, that the key to revival is the restoration of family. One glance at our culture, and it's easy to see how much the family has disintegrated over the last few decades. The number of fatherless households in America is shocking, and so it's no wonder that society is crumbling at an alarming rate. Malachi 4 speaks of a curse that will fall on the earth if parents and children do not turn their hearts towards one another, and it's fair to say that what we are seeing around us is a result of that curse.

However, this is not the last word in the story! We have a role to play in seeing the tide turn back to righteousness, as we press into a greater revelation of Jesus to be demonstrated through our families.

How awesome would it be to see fathers and mothers, and sons and daughters (both natural and spiritual) running together, ushering in the Kingdom of God to our cities and nations. Let's commit ourselves once again to being good fathers, mothers, sons, and daughters, and consecrate our families for the work of God on this earth.

Meditate on Genesis 18:19. Say it out loud a few times. Really think about how it applies to you. Ask yourself:

- Do I view my family as my mission field?
- Do I believe that my family has a call of God on it?

Ask the Holy Spirit:

- "Am I being intentional about demonstrating Your character through me towards my family?
- "Do I know what Your purposes are for my family?"
- "Even if there has been bad fruit in the past from my family line, do I believe You will redeem my family's purposes from this day forward?"

Write in your journal what you hear Him say.

Day 9 DEVOTIONAL PRAYER

"God, I consecrate my family, and set it aside for your glory. Give me faith and vision to believe that You have a call and purpose for my family to accomplish. Cleanse and wash away any curses brought on by sin and wrong agreements from past generations, and fill me and my family with your blessings. I choose to demonstrate honor, and show Your character through my actions and words, so that future generations may do the same. Let my family partner with You to bring righteousness and justice to the earth. So, today, I make the commitment that boldly says, "As for me and my house, we will serve the Lord!"

Declaration: My family's call and destiny is becoming aligned to God's purposes and set apart to bring Him glory.

Journal

"Worship must be Christ-centered, Holy Spirit led, a Response to the Father, about Intimacy and Service — and always lead to Transformation!"
Tim Hughes

Day 10

CONSECRATING OUR FINANCES

Honor the Lord with your wealth and with the firstfruits of all
your produce; then your barns will be filled with plenty, and
your vats will be bursting with wine.
(Proverbs 3:9-10, ESV)

THE PURSUIT OF MONEY HAS ENSLAVED more people than almost any other activity on this planet. Human history shows us the devastation to life and resources that is caused when man sets his desire on money. It's clear that Paul knew what he was talking about, when he wrote in 1 Timothy 6, "the love of money is the root of all kinds of evil." This is why it's so important that the children of God align themselves with Kingdom principles, submitting their finances, and how they are used, to the Lord.

Money and possessions are the second most referenced topic in the Bible. In fact, of the thirty-nine recorded parables that Jesus taught, eleven of them concern money. Does this mean that we as Christians should be consumed with material possessions and money? The short answer is an emphatic no! However, what we do with our finances can often be a good indicator of how much we trust the Lord and are submitted to Him. It can also be a good indicator of how much we take pride in our own accomplishments. Often people view the money they've accumulated as something they've gained on their own, thus feeling justified using their finances for whatever they want. Yes, they may give a few scraps to the church, or to some cause, but because they've taken credit for their own wealth, they don't acknowledge God's role in the process.

Deuteronomy 8:18 implores us to "remember the Lord your God, for it is He who gives you the ability to produce wealth." It's in this acknowledgement that we come to the realization that any wealth that we may have is a result of His blessing on our lives, and because of that, we are just stewards of the resources He has entrusted to us. If we are stewards, then we are responsible to be wise and effective with what He's given us. In this light, let's commit our finances to the purposes of God, and consecrate our money as a servant's tool that can be used to extend His Kingdom. Let's believe for His blessings to fall on us, so we can be a blessing to others.

Meditate on Proverbs 3:9-10. Say it out loud a few times. Really think about how it applies to you. Ask yourself:

- Do I honor God by the giving of my finances?
- Do I believe that my finances are my own, or are they God's?

Ask the Holy Spirit:

- "Have I trusted You with giving You my finances?
- "Have I asked You what I should be giving away, or am I just giving the bare minimum?"
- "Do I believe that You want to bless my finances so that I can bless others?"

Write in your journal what you hear Him say.

Day 10 DEVOTIONAL PRAYER

"God, I consecrate my finances to You, and I commit them to being used for Your glory and the extension of Your Kingdom. Forgive me for not acknowledging Your role in giving me the ability to gain wealth. Forgive me for viewing what You've given me as something for me to use as I wish, and not seeking Your guidance as to how my finances should be used. I choose to live a life of faith and generosity, instead of operating out of fear and an orphan spirit. As I trust You more in this area, I believe that You will bless me with more resources to help fund Your Kingdom. I believe that You are redeeming my poor financial choices of the past, and as I keep my eyes on You, You are setting me on a path of financial freedom and abundance."

Declaration: My finances are becoming an instrument of praise to God, and are consecrated to extend His Kingdom.

BECOMING FINANCES

"Spiritual transformation into Christ-likeness is not going to happen unless we act ... What transforms us is the will to obey Jesus Christ."
Dallas Willard

Day 11

REVELATION OF THE FATHER'S CREATIVITY

How many are your works, LORD! In wisdom you made them
all; the earth is full of your creatures.
(Psalm 104:24, NIV)

OD IS ALWAYS TRYING TO show us more of His character and
who He is, and one of the most amazing ways He's revealed
Himself is as our Father. Some may have a negative reaction
to the word "father," but this doesn't change the fact that God
wants to shift our perspective and demonstrate what a true Father really is. A godly identity is an important concept for us all to
understand, but we can't truly know our identity unless we get a redeemed view of who our Father in Heaven is. Besides seeing who He
is, we also need to hear His voice, because He longs for us to hear Him
speak His identity into us. Today, our Father wants to bring us into a
greater revelation of who He is, so that we can better understand who
we are to be. 1 John 4 tells us that in this world, we are like Him.

The Father is creative. In a single moment, He spoke the universe into existence, and what was created is more intricate and full
of life and color than we could ever comprehend. It seems every discovery science makes into the details of creation opens another door
where further details are waiting to be discovered. Infinite lifetimes
of searching God's creativity would not be enough to fully grasp the
vastness of who He is, and of His wonderful creation. In fact, from
His initial word, creation is still expanding and getting bigger. What's
also amazing is understanding that we were made in His image, so the
creativity residing inside the Father's heart also abides in us! God finds
pleasure watching His children create things that reflect His goodness
and nature.

For example, God so values creativity that the first time the Bible
speaks of God's Spirit filling a man is found in Exodus 35, where we

learn that a man named Bezalel was anointed for the express purpose of creating artistic design in gold, silver, bronze, stones, and wood. Knowing that our God has created us with the intent of us reflecting His nature, it's important that we grasp the significance of our actions and words, and what is created because of those choices. Just as words can be used to create life and death, the things we create in our lifetimes can be used to bring God glory, or defame His name. Let's choose to walk in our Father's footsteps, and create life with our words and deeds.

Meditate on Psalm 104:24. Say it out loud a few times. Really think about how it applies to you. Ask yourself:

- Do I struggle with using the word Father, in relation to God?
- Do I allow the Father to speak His identity into me?

Ask the Holy Spirit:

- "Do I find myself admiring Your creativity?"
- "Do I allow You to influence my creativity?"
- "Have the things that I've created brought glory to You?"

Write in your journal what you hear Him say.

Day 11 DEVOTIONAL PRAYER

"Father, thank You for breathing Your identity into me. Thank You for making me a reflection of who You are. Thank You for Your wonderful creation, and that I have the honor and joy to explore the things You've made. Thank You that You've made me to be creative, just like You. Forgive me for using my creativity to make things that do not bring You honor. I choose to use my words and actions wisely, to create things that build up, create life, and exalt Your name. Thank You that I have been anointed to use my gift of creativity to extend Your Kingdom, and to demonstrate Your character and goodness."

Declaration: I am becoming more like my Father and using my creativity to bring life-giving answers and solutions to the world around me.

Journal

"Trusting Christ for salvation but resisting transformation. We occasionally flip the switch, but most of the time we settle for shadows."
Max Lucado

Day 12

REVELATION OF THE FATHER'S LOVE

"See how very much our Father loves us, for He calls us His children, and that is what we are! But the people who belong to this world don't recognize that we are God's children because they don't know Him." (1 John 3:1, NLT)

OUR ENGLISH WORD "LOVE" IS WEIRD. For such a complex subject to be relegated to a single four-letter word seems a bit ludicrous. We use the same word to describe an affinity towards ice cream, a sexual desire, or our response to God. This is why it's helpful to look at love from a different language's perspective. The New Testament was mostly written in Greek, and because of this, it's important to look at how the Greeks used words that we interpret as love. The Bible uses four different Greek words that we interpret as love – *storge*, which is a familial love that usually flows both ways; *philio*, which speaks of a deep emotional connection, whether it's to a friend or chocolate; *eros*, which is sexual in nature; and *agape*, which is the type of love that God shows us, and the type of love that He asks us to show others.

The Father is love. He doesn't just love us, He is love. He doesn't demonstrate His love towards us because we deserve it or have done something for Him, but He shows His love to us because that is who He is. His nature is to give Himself away, without regards to Himself. He loves you as much today as He did before you chose to walk after Him. Not only has our Father demonstrated His love in this manner, He's asked us to do the same to Him and to our fellow man. Culture has cheapened the word love to mean something that is self-referential, and is only given because of what the person receiving the love does back to the giver. This type of "love" has created a culture that uses people and spits them out when they've served their purpose. So in a world that demonstrates this type of love, the Father is asking

His children to become counter-cultural, and to show what love is truly supposed to look like. But this can only happen if we have an encounter with God's love, and begin walking in His character. So let's ask and believe for a fresh revelation of the Father's love, so we can demonstrate His loving nature to the world around us, and bring change to a world that is in desperate need of *agape*.

Meditate on 1 John 3:1. Say it out loud a few times. Really think about how it applies to you. Ask yourself:

- Do I love others with conditions?
- Do I truly believe that God loves me unconditionally?

Ask the Holy Spirit:

- "Do I know what it means to be truly loved?"
- "Do You love me unconditionally?"
- "Do I demonstrate Your love towards others, or do I still show a love that has hooks of expectation?"

Write in your journal what you hear Him say.

Day 12 DEVOTIONAL PRAYER

"Father, I thank You for the way You show Your love towards me. It's hard to grasp how deeply You love me, and are passionate about who I am. I recognize that it's often difficult to receive this type of love, because of the lies of the enemy I've entertained. Forgive me for listening to fear and doubt, and cleanse me from all agreements that I've made with them. Show me more of who You are, and the way You love. Let Your character fill me to overflowing, so that I may love both You and others the same way that You love me. I choose to give love without an expectation of getting anything in return. I choose to give love completely for the benefit of the one receiving it. Thank You that Your love is eternal, and I choose today to let that love transform my life and be shown through every word and action I make."

Declaration: I am becoming love, and demonstrating *agape* to a broken world in need of a revelation of how the Father loves.

Journal

"I have seen miracles in my time, my brothers and sisters. The greatest miracle of all, I believe, is the transformation that comes into the life of a man or a woman who accepts the restored gospel of Jesus Christ and tries to live it in his or her life."
Gordon B. Hinckley

Day 13

REVELATION OF THE FATHER'S GOODNESS

Whatever is good and perfect is a gift coming down to us
from God our Father, who created all the lights in the heav-
ens. He never changes or casts a shifting shadow.
(James 1:17, NLT)

*I*N JUST ABOUT EVERY CHURCH across America, we could stand
on a stage and proclaim the words, "God is good," and we would
immediately get a response from the entire room, "All the time!"
Then we would say, "All the time," with the room responding,
"God is good!"

This has become one of those "Christianese" sayings that is often
said, but not always believed. Oh, sure, we may not say out loud that
God isn't good all the time, but in reality, we've all gone through experiences where it felt as if we've been abandoned. This is where we need
to allow truth to trump feelings. Satan's temptation to Eve in the garden, was to entice her to know more. The word, "know" is the Hebrew
word yada, and it's the same word used when the Bible says that Adam
knew Eve, and she conceived a child. It's not a passive informational
type of knowledge, but an intimate knowing.

The enemy still tempts us the same way, trying to get us to bond
with our negative experiences and the associated feelings, so that we
allow fear and doubt to weave around our thoughts and decisions. But
the Father's invitation is for us to yada Him. He's asking us to experience Him in both good and difficult times, so that our thoughts go
through the grid of His goodness, versus our thoughts going through
the filter of hurt.

The fact is that God is good, and His purposes for us are good.
Jeremiah 29:11 says, "For I know the plans I have for you," declares
the Lord, "plans to prosper you and not to harm you, plans to give you
hope and a future." We can rest on His promises such as Romans 8:28,
which says "all things work together for those who love Him, and are

called according to His purposes." We need to stay vigilant in not allowing the enemy's temptation of disappointment to cause us to doubt God's goodness. Instead, we need to run into the loving arms of the Father, so that we can experience His goodness, and live a fear-free life of confidence, knowing that He has us in His hands.

Meditate on James 1:17. Say it out loud a few times. Really think about how it applies to you. Ask yourself:

- Have I allowed negative experiences affect how I view God?
- Do I still have fear and doubt for the future?

Ask the Holy Spirit:

- "Do I believe that You want to give me good gifts?"
- "Do I have the peace and faith to believe that You are good all the time"
- "Have I bonded with my pain versus bonding with You during painful times?"

Write in your journal what you hear Him say.

Day 13 DEVOTIONAL PRAYER

"Father, I confess that I may say the words, "You are good," but sometimes the hurts that I've bonded with keep me from believing in Your goodness. Forgive me for listening to the lies of the enemy that have brought on fear and doubt. I choose to walk away from those agreements. I ask for a fresh revelation of Your character, so that I can experience Your goodness in a new way. I choose to look to You during difficult times, and I ask for You to give me peace and faith to walk through storms with a courage that knows You are working all things together. Thank You for your blessings on my life. Thank You for provision, and for Your faithfulness. I pray that I will always remember Your great love, and that You have great plans for my life. I choose to believe that You are good all the time!"

Declaration: I am becoming one who believes in the goodness of God in every situation, and does not entertain doubt or fear.

Journal

"Give up the struggle and the fight; relax in the omnipotence of the Lord Jesus; look up into His lovely face and as you behold Him, He will transform you into His likeness. You do the beholding — He does the transforming. There is no short-cut to holiness."
Alan Redpath

Day 14

REVELATION OF THE FATHER'S GRACE & MERCY

Let us then with confidence draw near to the throne of grace, that we may receive mercy and find grace to help in time of need. (Hebrews 4:16, ESV)

ANY PEOPLE LIVE IN A perpetual state of fear, because they aren't convinced of God's mercy for their lives. They may be dealing with addiction, or pride, or any number of other issues, and every time these things come up, they fall into the same cycle of fear and doubt, not having confidence in the Father's mercy, nor the grace that He's releasing to take on more of His character. Because of this shame, they often put up barriers in their mind and create a separation that's not really there.

One of the most misunderstood concepts in Christianity is the difference between grace and mercy. Often times, people use these words interchangeably, not understanding the power and uniqueness in how both of them operate. Many of us are familiar with the term "loose grace," which is used to describe the idea that because of God's unending grace, we can do whatever we want and still be in good standing with Him. It's true that God's grace is never ending, but does that really mean we can take advantage of it and live like hell? We can only have boldness to enter into God's presence because of His grace, but our right standing with God is only given because of His mercy. Mercy says that, even though I deserve to die because of sin, it's through the death and resurrection of Jesus that the Father has freely pardoned my debts and invited me into relationship. Grace, on the other hand, is not about pardoning sins, but it is about the empowerment that God gives us to receive His mercy and walk in righteousness. God's all-sufficient grace is given so that we can be more like Christ, not live in more sin.

So, if someone says that they are free to do whatever they want because of God's grace, they are essentially spitting in the face of Jesus's sacrifice on the cross, therefore denying the very reason God's grace is given. 1 Peter 1 says that God's mercy has caused us to be born again and to possess a living hope. It's this hope of right standing with God that gives us confidence to know that His grace is empowering us to become more like Him, and to let the old selfish life die. His grace and mercy gives us boldness to know that we can always go to Him and receive His love.

Meditate on Hebrews 4:16. Say it out loud a few times. Really think about how it applies to you. Ask yourself:

- Do I understand the difference between grace and mercy?

- Have I abused the concept of God's mercy to live a selfish life?

Ask the Holy Spirit:

- "Do I still hold on to fear and believe the lie that Your mercy is not covering me?"

- "Do I have confidence to approach You?"

- "Do I walk in Your grace that empowers me to turn away sinfulness, and follows You into righteousness?"

Write in your journal what you hear Him say.

Day 14 DEVOTIONAL PRAYER

"Father, I thank You so much for the grace and mercy that You have shown me. Thank You that through Jesus, I can have right-standing with You and receive Your mercy which washes away all my sins. Thank You that Your grace empowers me to walk a more righteous life, and to take on more of Your character. Forgive me for believing the lie that Your grace is given for me to live however I wish. Forgive me for my selfishness and for not acknowledging what Your sacrifice on the cross was for. I receive Your grace that gives me boldness to come before You, and to be Your representative on this earth. Let me never forget Your mercy, and let me never walk without Your grace."

Declaration: I am one who is becoming dependent on the grace of God and who is thankful for His mercy on my life.

"The same Jesus who turned water into wine can transform your home, your life, your family, and your future. He is still in the miracle-working business, and His business is the business of transformation."
Adrian Rogers

Day 15

REVELATION OF THE FATHER'S RIGHTEOUSNESS

"Righteous Father, though the world does not know you, I know you, and they know that you have sent me. I have made you known to them, and will continue to make you known in order that the love you have for me may be in them and that I myself may be in them." (John 17:25-26, NIV)

THIS WORLD IS CONSUMED WITH JUSTICE. It seems just about every other day, another social justice organization is trying to make the world aware of the latest disadvantaged people group that need rescuing. Yes, there's injustice in the world. But identifying the root of those injustices and how those things can be dealt with is something humanistic thinking tries desperately to solve, but never gets right. Their normal solutions usually involve taking things away from one group to give to another group. This type of "justice" ends up pitting people group against people group, and can often cause a greater injustice than the original offense. The reason that all these man-made ideas never succeed is because none of them are rooted in God's justice, which is the same as His righteousness. In the above Scripture, Jesus calls the Father "Righteous Father," which is a revelation of a part of the Father's character. In the same Scripture, Jesus acknowledges that the world does not know the Father, but His goal was to bring that revelation of the Father to us.

In both the Hebrew Old Testament, and Greek New Testament, the words righteousness and justice are the same word, and are very rarely interpreted as something different. This should tell us something about our perceptions of those words.

First, you cannot separate God's righteousness from His justice. Isaiah 5:16 says, "But the Lord of hosts is exalted in justice, and the Holy God shows himself holy in righteousness." Also, true justice looks like righteousness, which speaks of the proper alignment of all things to God's character and nature. Finally, when God makes righ-

71

teous judgements, it will always bring proper alignment and justice, as well as demonstrate His goodness and love. It's interesting to note that John 5:22 records Jesus saying, "the Father judges no one, but has entrusted all judgment to the Son." However, because Jesus also said that He only does what He sees the Father doing, we can be confident that the righteous judgements of Jesus will always reflect the character and nature of the Father. Because of this, if the goodness and love of God are not present in someone's idea of what justice looks like, that idea is false, and will not bring about righteousness.

Meditate on John 17:25-26. Say it out loud a few times. Really think about how it applies to you. Ask yourself:
- Have I used human reasoning to form my ideas of what justice looks like?
- Have I separated justice from righteousness?

Ask the Holy Spirit:
- "Am I inviting You to show me what righteousness looks like?"
- "Have I given you permission to form my ideas of what justice is?"
- "Does God's righteousness seem like something that I can walk in?"

Write in your journal what you hear Him say.

Day 15 DEVOTIONAL PRAYER

"Father, You are the Righteous One! You are bringing all things into proper alignment to Your righteousness, so that true justice will be seen in the world. Forgive me for listening to what human thinking says about justice, and forgive me for not allowing You to form my opinions on how to better display your righteousness and justice. Your judgements are not something to be feared, but they are something to be delighted in, because they will always reflect Your nature of goodness and love. Let my life better reflect who You are, and use me to bring proper alignment and righteousness to my family, my church, my work, my friendships, and every other place You send me."

Declaration: I am one who submits my idea of what righteousness is to God, and believes that His justice is always best.

Journal

"To renew your mind is to involve yourself in the process of allowing God to bring to the surface the lies you have mistakenly accepted and replace them with truth. To the degree that you do this, your behavior will be transformed."
Charles Stanley

Day 16

WHO THE FATHER SAYS WE ARE

Because you are sons, God has sent forth the Spirit of His
Son into our hearts, crying, "Abba! Father!" Therefore you
are no longer a slave, but a son and if a son, then an heir
through God. (Galatians 4:6-7, NASB)

I T's ALWAYS AMAZING TO SEE how often our children take on our mannerisms, and sound like us when they talk. It can bring joy when they display some of our good characteristics, but it can be very eye-opening when they start looking or sounding like some of our less-than-flattering attributes! Regardless, it's a good reminder that children are designed to look and sound like their parents.

The last several days, we've been meditating on the Father's creativity, love, goodness, grace, mercy, and righteousness, which are more than simple descriptors of who He is, but are a part of His very essence. When we grab hold of the revelations of the Father's attributes, we can begin to see who we are called to be. Jesus is the exact representation of the Father in all ways. As a Son, he only did what He saw the Father doing and He was fully like him in behavior, thought, speech, and attitude. As we are sons and daughters of God, in Christ Jesus, the Father is inviting us into the same process of becoming like Him. In Christ, we share in His inheritance, which is entering completely into the fullness of God. Regardless of our current circumstance, we must never forget that we are sons and daughters of God. The blood of Jesus and the gift of the Holy Spirit testify to our hearts that we are a new creation, so we can have confidence in who we are and who our Father is.

Sons and daughters act differently than mere servants. Sons and daughters are invested in the family and understand that they have a role to play in the success of the family business, which in our case is seeing God's Kingdom extended and established in the earth. Sons and daughters look like their Father: They walk in boldness and confidence knowing their delegated authority and commission. Who the Father is to you will be how the Father is demonstrated through you. As others look at your life, they should be able to read the message of the Father's love and goodness through your actions.

Meditate on Galatians 4:6-7. Say it out loud a few times. Really think about how it applies to you. Ask yourself:

- Do I live my life like a son or daughter or more like an orphan?
- What message of the Father are others reading through my life?

Ask the Holy Spirit:

- "Are there any lies that I believe that are keeping me from relating to God as a Father?"
- "Where in my life am I acting like an orphan instead of a son or daughter?"
- "Do I walk with confidence and boldness in my identity, or fear and timidity?"

Write in your journal what you hear Him say.

Day 16 DEVOTIONAL PRAYER

"Father, thank You for Your unending love towards me. Thank You for the blood of Your Son, that reconciles me to You not as a slave, but as a son. Thank You for the Holy Spirit, who has made me alive in You, allowing me to know You as my Father. I repent for not always believing that You love me. I ask you to renew my mind that I would begin to relate to You as a son and not as an orphan. God, change my heart; bring my heart into alignment with Yours. Let me see as You see, love as You love, and live as You live. I receive Your grace and now come boldly before You, leaving fear drowned in Your love. Thank you Father, for making me into a living, breathing message of Your love and goodness to the world around me."

Declaration: My identity is found in God, and I'm becoming a much-loved child who is about my Father's business.

Journal

_____

_____

_____

_____

_____

_____

_____

_____

_____

_____

_____

_____

_____

_____

_____

_____

"The God who can change a sinner into a Christian by giving him His life can equally transform the fleshly Christian into a spiritual one by giving him His life more abundantly."
Watchman Nee

Day 17

REVELATION OF THE BLOOD OF JESUS

But now you have been united with Christ Jesus. Once you were far away from God, but now you have been brought near to Him through the blood of Christ. (Ephesians 2:13, NLT)

E HAVE JUST FINISHED DIVING into a greater revelation of the Father's character and nature. Just as it is vitally important for us to grasp who the Father is, we must also understand who Jesus is, and who we are in Him. Many people create a picture of Jesus in their mind, but unfortunately this often creates a false idea of who He really is. When we create a Jesus who is the way we want Him to be (and who often looks and sounds like us), instead of getting revelation of the true Son of God, we get a revelation of ourselves in the form of Jesus. So, for the next few days, we're going to lay aside all our preconceived ideas and press into knowing Jesus in a greater measure, letting His glory be revealed to us.

When John the Baptist saw Jesus, he declared, "Behold the Lamb of God who takes away the sins of the world" (John 1:29, 36). One of Jesus's titles is "Lamb of God." This isn't just a cute little name used in a children's song, but it is full of impact and meaning for us as followers of Christ. On the cross, Jesus literally became a sacrifice of atonement for our sins. He was as a "lamb to the slaughter" for the purpose of establishing a new way to the Father for us, so we would be reconciled to Him. Through His shed blood, Jesus redeemed (purchased) us from the law of sin, and by His love and grace brought us back into right relationship with the Father. His blood is the guarantee of the forgiveness of our sins, and we have been freed from those sins in order to live an abundant life in Christ Jesus (John 10:10).

The blood of Jesus is not only the payment for our sins, but his blood is the seal of a new covenant that we have entered into with the Father. By believing and confessing Jesus as our Savior and Lord,

His blood has cleansed us and re-covered us in His glory. We now can enter boldly into His throne room and commune with Him. This new covenant is a covenant of love and grace where mercy triumphs over judgement; a blood covenant that says that by His stripes we are healed and whole in every part of our being; a covenant of abundant life instead of death. Jesus's blood broke the curse of sin and death and introduced us into a life of freedom in Him. Wow! What a precious gift.

Meditate on Ephesians 2:13. Say it out loud a few times. Really think about how it applies to you. Ask yourself:

- Do I understand the significance of the blood of Jesus?
- How does the blood of Jesus bring me closer to the Father?

Ask the Holy Spirit:

- "Do I believe that the blood of Jesus has washed away my sins?"
- "Am I allowing You to lead me to the truth of Jesus?"
- "How do I walk in a greater revelation of the power of the blood of Jesus?"

Write in your journal what you hear Him say.

Day 17 DEVOTIONAL PRAYER

"Jesus, my Lord and Savior, thank You for making a way for me to become reconciled to the Father. Thank You for loving me so much, that you gave Your life in exchange for mine. Thank You for shedding your blood for my sins and cleansing me completely. Lord, help me to continually walk in the freedom You purchased for me with Your blood. I choose to serve You, and walk in a greater revelation of the power and authority that is in Your blood. For Your glory and honor!"

Declaration: I am becoming closer to God because of the blood of Jesus that has cleansed me and empowered me to walk in His power.

Journal

*"Holiness consists of three things —
separation from sin, dedication to God,
transformation into Christ's image. It is in
vain that we talk about the last, unless
we know something experimentally
about the first."*
James H. Aughey

Day 18

REVELATION OF JESUS AS THE BREAD OF LIFE

Then Jesus declared, "I am the bread of life. Whoever comes to me will never go hungry, and whoever believes in me will never be thirsty." (John 6:35, NIV)

ALMOST EVERY CULTURE in the world has a form of bread as a staple of their diet. Is there anything better than a good piece of sourdough, eaten with a nice meal? Think about a warm baguette, slathered in butter, or doused with oil and vinegar. As good as that sounds, Jesus is inviting us into a relationship with Him where He becomes the sustenance of our lives. Just as we rely on food and water to nourish our physical beings, Jesus is inviting us to feast on Him to nourish our spirits and souls.

John 6 records a conversation between Jesus and His disciples in which Jesus makes a statement that He is the Bread of Life. This was right after the disciples discussed the miraculous provision of manna God gave Israel in the desert, and then asked Jesus for a sign so they could believe He was who He said He was. We can see in the gospels how many signs, wonders, and miracles the disciples saw Jesus perform, but here they were, asking for another sign.

Jesus did not oblige them. Instead, He introduced them to the concept of living a daily life in Him, versus relying on an occasional supernatural experience.

I think we've all found ourselves at one time or another hoping for that one spiritual experience that we can grab ahold of and sustain us until the next miraculous moment comes our way. But is that really the type of life Jesus is wanting for us? Instead, isn't He asking us to trust in Him and dine on Him every hour of every day? The cross has made a way for us so we do not have to rely on a couple of religious experiences, scattered throughout our lifetimes. Instead, we are welcomed into a daily walk with the risen King Jesus. His invitation is for us to go past an occasional spiritual experience, and into the arms of a personal Savior, who wants us to know Him and become more like Him. It's in this type of relationship that we truly will never hunger or thirst again.

Meditate on John 6:35. Say it out loud a few times. Really think about how it applies to you. Ask yourself:

- Do I really believe that Jesus wants a daily relationship with me?
- Have I tried to sustain my life through spiritual experiences or through a relationship with God?

Ask the Holy Spirit:

- "Am I hungering after You or a spiritual experience?"
- "Am I seeking after You on a daily basis?"
- "Are my spirit and soul being sustained by You or something else?"

Write in your journal what you hear Him say.

Day 18 DEVOTIONAL PRAYER

"Jesus, I thank You that Your death and resurrection has made a way for me to know You more. I thank You that the old veil of separation is no longer there, and You have invited me into a daily relationship with You. Forgive me for keeping the veil between us. Forgive me for relying on spiritual experiences to nourish me, instead of feasting off the love, joy, and peace that is found in Your heart. I choose to invite You into every part of my day, so that I can know You more, and take on more of Your character. I choose to find my sustenance in You, and I know that I will no longer hunger and thirst for impersonal spiritual experiences, because I know that those are a counterfeit to what is found in Your heart."

Declaration: I am becoming one who is sustained by the presence of God and is inviting Him into every moment of every day.

"Your psychological orientation is past and present but God's orientation is future. Transformation doesn't happen because of the past. There is nothing in the butterfly's past that can make it fly."
Mark J. Chironna

Day 19

REVELATION OF JESUS AS THE WAY, TRUTH, AND LIFE

Jesus answered, "I am the way and the truth and the life. No one comes to the Father except through me. If you really know me, you will know my Father as well. From now on, you do know Him and have seen Him." (John 14:6-7, NIV)

THIS MAY SOUND OVERLY SIMPLISTIC, but doorways are used to get to places that, without their use, could not be otherwise accessed. In a world that says that there are many doorways to God, Jesus makes the statement to His disciples that He is the only way to the Father. In a world that says we all have our own truth, over 2,000 years ago Jesus said He is the doorway to truth. And in a world consumed with selfishness, true life can only be found by saying "yes" to the invitation of Jesus to live in Him. Ephesians 2:6 says that our spirits are currently seated next to God in heavenly places, because we are found in Christ. This type of access to God was an unthinkable concept to anyone before Jesus came along, and because of His invitation, we can dwell in the presence of God.

There has never been a time where so much information is instantly available to most of the world, and yet, we also live in a time where so much mass deception is everywhere. It is pretty easy to conclude that information doesn't necessarily equal truth. That is why it's a false statement to say that there are many truths, because truth isn't information, it's a Person – Jesus! This is also why we need to be found in Jesus, so that we can live in truth, and recognize deception when it comes.

The world is obsessed with living for itself. People are engaged in a non-stop life singularly focused on gaining more for themselves, willing to do just about anything to get ahead. This is an exhausting type of life that, regardless of how much is gained, will never be satisfied. However, if our focus shifts from living for ourselves to living for Christ, we now have access to all that God has, because we are about our Father's business. This type of life does not worry about provision, because God has already promised it. It doesn't run away from hardships, but recognizes difficult times as opportunities to grow in character. It finds joy in giving itself away to its fellow neighbor, so that others can experience the love and goodness of God through a laid-down life.

Meditate on John 14:6-7. Say it out loud a few times. Really think about how it applies to you. Ask yourself:
- Have I believed the lie that says we all have our own truth?
- Have I lived my life for myself?

Ask the Holy Spirit:
- "Do I believe that You have seated me, in Christ, next to the Father?"
- "Am I seeking my own truth, or am I inviting You into my thoughts and mindsets?"
- "Am I giving the way I live my life to You for Your glory?"

Write in your journal what you hear Him say.

Day 19 DEVOTIONAL PRAYER

"Jesus, I thank You that You are the way, the truth, and the life. Thank You that You have revealed the Father to me, and that I am seated with You in heavenly places. Forgive me for trying to find ways to God that were not found in You. I walk away from all those other things that I placed in front of You, and I choose to live my life in and for You. I'm sorry for listening to the lie that I have my own truth. So instead, I choose to only look to You for truth, because You are Truth. Forgive me for living for myself, and having my own interests at the forefront of my thoughts. I walk away from that type of living, and I choose to live my life for You, and for Your glory. Let my entire life be found in You."

<u>Declaration</u>: I am becoming aligned to living in the truth of Jesus so that I am less prone to believing lies and deception.

Journal

"It is the Gospel that can translate you from darkness into light...Only the gospel can cause a transformation."
Benson Andrew Idahosa

REVELATION OF JESUS AS THE GOOD SHEPHERD

"I am the good shepherd; I know my own sheep, and they know me, just as my Father knows me, and I know the Father. So I sacrifice my life for the sheep." (John 10:14-15, NLT)

ID YOU KNOW THAT SHEEP only respond to their respective shepherd? If you take two flocks of sheep that have different shepherds and put them all together in the same pen, and one of the shepherds goes into the pen and calls the sheep, only the flock that knows that particular shepherd's voice will come to him. The other shepherd's flock will ignore the call entirely because they do not recognize the voice calling them. In the same way, we are called to know our Shepherd's voice, so that His voice is the only voice we listen to.

Jesus stated that He is the Good Shepherd. A shepherd intimately cares for his flock. He knows how to differentiate one sheep from the other, and he recognizes the personalities of each one and what type of care they need. A shepherd diligently keeps watch over his sheep, and is careful to keep them out of trouble; he binds up their wounds, is faithful to feed and water them, and diligently leads them to a safe place to graze. A good shepherd lays down his life for his sheep, spending his time and energy—sacrificing even his physical body—to make sure they are cared for. Jesus demonstrated the actions of a good shepherd by laying His life down for us, that we might live abundantly. In Psalm 23 David paints an awesome picture of how the Lord is our Shepherd.

"The Lord is my shepherd, I have all that I need. He lets me rest in green meadows, he leads me beside peaceful streams. He renews my strength. He guides me along right paths, bringing honor to his name. Even when I walk through the darkest valley, I will not be afraid, for you are close beside me. Your rod and your staff protect and comfort me. You prepare a feast for me in the presence of my enemies. You honor me by anointing my head with oil. My cup overflows with blessings. Surely your goodness and unfailing love will pursue me all the days of my life, And I will live in the house of the Lord forever."

We must learn to not only be sheep led by our Good Shepherd, knowing his voice and obeying it, but we must also grow up to become shepherds like Him and care for others with the same heart of love that He demonstrated to us – a life laid down for the sake of others.

Meditate on John 10:14-15. Say it out loud a few times. Really think about how it applies to you. Ask yourself:

- Do I know what it means for Jesus to be my Good Shepherd?
- Do I trust Jesus to take care of me?

Ask the Holy Spirit:

- "Will you please teach me to know Your voice?"
- "What are some of the voices that I have been listening to over Yours?"
- "If there are any places where I have heard Your voice, but not obeyed, please reveal it to me."

Write in your journal what you hear Him say.

Day 20 DEVOTIONAL PRAYER

"Lord, thank You for being my Good Shepherd. Thank You for leading me and guiding me into places of provision and safety. Jesus, I repent for not trusting You, even though I know You have my best at heart. I place my gaze back on You and look to You to lead and guide me. Thank You for your faithfulness and lovingkindness towards me. Teach me to love others the way that You have loved me. I want to know You more, and I want to trust You and walk in Your ways. Jesus, give me a humble heart, that I would follow You all the days of my life."

Declaration: I am becoming in tune with hearing the voice of Jesus and resting in His arms of protection.

Journal

_____

_____

_____

_____

_____

_____

_____

_____

_____

_____

_____

_____

_____

_____

_____

_____

_____

"The key to transformation is to love the learning, and above all, enjoy the process of becoming who you really are in Jesus."
Graham Cooke

Day 21

REVELATION OF JESUS AS A SERVANT

"For even the Son of Man did not come to be served, but to
serve, and to give His life a ransom for many."
(Mark 10:45, NASB)

T HE KINGDOM OF HEAVEN is upside down compared to the
kingdoms of this world. The logical human mind, apart from
God, is always looking for ways to advance itself and to gain
power and recognition through works. So many people find
their identity in what they do. Take a moment and think back to a
time when you were at a social gathering and people were introduc-
ing themselves to each other. They almost always start off giving their
name, and then proceed to identify themselves by the kind of work
they do. If they don't, it will almost certainly be the first question asked
of them.

The world has made work our identity and our stepping-stone to
influence. Jesus, however, took that and flipped it on its head. Imagine
the disciples hanging out and all of a sudden a discussion (more like
an argument!) erupts, as to who is the greatest in the kingdom. They all
have done work they perceive as prominent, seemingly earning themselves the title of the greatest in the Kingdom. But Jesus tells them,
if you want to be great in the Kingdom of God, you must become a
servant of all. What? A servant is the least in social standing, yet this
is who Jesus likens to the greatest. Talk about culture shock.

The life of Jesus was marked by servanthood. His disciples watched
in astonishment as he knelt and washed their feet at their last meal together. Later, we see him in the Garden of Gethsemane praying to the
Father, knowing what was about to happen to Him, and at the end of
His prayer, the heart of the bond-servant pours from Jesus as he says,
"not my will, but yours be done." A bond-servant is one who serves not

because he has to, but because he chooses to out of love. We have been given the same commission on the earth that Jesus had. If we truly want to follow His example, our lives will demonstrate both serving our Father in heaven, and the people around us.

Meditate on Mark 10:45. Say it out loud a few times. Really think about how it applies to you. Ask yourself:

- Do I notice the needs of other people around me?
- Am I actively serving other people?

Ask the Holy Spirit:

- "Do I have the heart of a servant?"
- "When I serve others do I do it out of love or out of duty and obligation?"
- "What does it look like for me to have the same servant heart as Jesus in my everyday life?"

Write in your journal what you hear Him say.

Day 21 DEVOTIONAL PRAYER

"Lord, thank You for demonstrating a servant's heart, motivated by love. That love was so great, You even chose to die on the cross for me. Help me to be motivated by love. Let the outworking of that love lead me to serve others. I ask that You soften any places in my heart that have become hardened to others or void of compassion. Fill me to overflowing with Your oil of gladness, that I might joyfully serve others and demonstrate Your love and Kingdom to the world around me."

Declaration: I am becoming more like Jesus every day and living a life of service to both God and my fellow man.

Journal

"The only true worship is extreme worship, and only extreme worship brings extreme results — transformation."
Bill Johnson

Day 22

REVELATION OF JESUS AND HIS GIFTS TO US

But to each one of us grace was given according to the measure of Christ's gift. And He Himself gave some to be apostles, some prophets, some evangelists, and some pastors and teachers. (Eph 4:7, 11 NKJV)

A T SOME POINT WE'VE ALL given a gift, or have been the recipient of a gift, that consisted of personal time coupons to be redeemed at the receiver's leisure. These coupons could range from the giver providing yardwork, to cooking a meal, or even giving a backrub. When we were younger, we thought that these types of coupons were a little bit of a cop-out to providing a "real" gift. But the older we've gotten, the more we have come to realize that these types of gifts are much more valuable, as they represent our time, and who we are.

Many of us are familiar with the gifts of Jesus that are listed in Ephesians 4, which are often labeled as the five-fold gifts. We like to look at these gifts as Jesus's coupons of Himself, given to us. Now, there's not enough time to really dive into the depths of these gifts, and how they function, especially because there are a lot of differing opinions on how they work, but most everyone can agree that the purpose of these gifts are, as verse 12 states, "for the equipping of the saints for the work of ministry, for the edifying of the body of Christ."

When Paul wrote his letter to the Ephesians, he wasn't writing it just to the leaders of the church; he was writing it to all believers. So, when he says that each of us is given a grace for these gifts, it includes all of us. Jesus isn't merely handing out impersonal gifts indiscriminately, He's giving the gift of Himself to be shown through you and me. His invitation is for us to be His representatives on earth, and bring His perspective and character to every part of the world. Equipping the saints, and edifying the body of Christ, isn't just something that is done at church gatherings, or in a classroom setting; it can also be done in a coffee shop with a friend, or at home with your children, or any other place that life finds us. Wherever people are being built up in Christ, equipping and edification is happening. So, it's okay if we don't necessarily view ourselves with the titles of apostle, prophet, evangelist, pastor, or teacher, because it's not about titles anyway. We must realize that those things are being displayed when we let Jesus demonstrate Himself through our lives. It's through our "yes" to Jesus, and our partnership with Him, that His gifts are shown.

Meditate on Ephesians 4:7&11. Say it out loud a few times. Really think about how it applies to you. Ask yourself:

- Do I believe that Jesus has given me a gift?
- Do I view these gifts as something I use by myself, or something I use with Him?

Ask the Holy Spirit:

- "What is the gift of Jesus that He has given to me?"
- "Do I intentionally display the gift of Jesus in me towards others?"
- "Do I believe that You can use my life to equip others and build up the body of Christ?"

Write in your journal what you hear Him say.

Day 22 DEVOTIONAL PRAYER

"Jesus, I thank You for the life You lived, and the way You demonstrated how to be the best apostle, prophet, evangelist, pastor, and teacher. I'm humbled that You choose to display who You are through me, and I thank You for the gift that You've placed on my life to be displayed to others. Forgive me for not believing that You've gifted me with significance. Also, forgive me for viewing Your gifts as impersonal items that I get to use, instead of understanding that the gift is You, through me. Give me the grace to build up and equip my fellow brothers and sisters, and to help them draw closer to You through the gifting that You've place in me. Thank You for giving Yourself to me."

Declaration: I am becoming more of who I was created to be by demonstrating the character of Jesus to those around me.

Journal

BECOMING GIFTS

"He is intangible and invisible. But His work is more powerful than the most ferocious wind. The Spirit brings order out of chaos and beauty out of ugliness. He can transform a sin-blistered man into a paragon of virtue. The Spirit changes people. The Author of life is also the Transformer of life."
R.C. Sproul

Day 23

REVELATION OF THE LIVING WATER OF THE HOLY SPIRIT

"He who believes in Me, as the Scripture has said, out of his heart will flow rivers of living water." But this He spoke concerning the Spirit, whom those believing in Him would receive.
(John 7:38-39, NKJV)

W E HAVE ALL EXPERIENCED those times in our lives where we've felt dry and not very "close" to God. Of course, we know that God does not leave us or forsake us, so those feelings do not reflect reality. In fact, the truth is that we are never dry, because Jesus promised to those who believe in Him, that the Holy Spirit will flow out of them like living waters. The gospel of John records that Jesus stood up and shouted that statement to the people during the height of a festival — the Feast of Tabernacles, which was a celebration of God's deliverance out of Egypt, and was a recognition of His salvation, shelter, provision, and trustworthiness. As part of the activities, the priests would draw water out of the pool of Siloam, and proceed to the temple to pour the water out onto the altar. This was done to demonstrate the prophecies found in Ezekiel 47 and Zechariah 14, which spoke of waters flowing out of the temple. But, just as Jesus so often did, He turned this old religious demonstration on its head, and introduced a completely new way of thinking. This new paradigm no longer relies on a physical place — the temple — to be the source of God's glory being demonstrated, but now, all those who believe in Christ are the temple of the Lord in which those living waters are poured out.

The purpose of these living waters is spoken of in Zechariah 14:9: "And the Lord will be king over all the earth. On that day there will be one Lord—his name alone will be worshiped." The living waters are also about the fulfillment of Habakkuk 2:14, which says, "For the earth will be filled with the knowledge of the glory of the Lord as the waters cover the sea." Notice in this verse that His glory is already covering the earth, but it's the knowledge of this glory that is being prophesied. The Holy Spirit empowers us, and flows out of us with His living waters, so that the earth will experience Him and His glory. As God's sons and daughters, our commission is to release the living waters out of our lives into every place we go, so that the earth will become transformed with His glory.

Meditate on John 7:38-39. Say it out loud a few times. Really think about how it applies to you. Ask yourself:

- Do I believe that there are living waters inside of me?
- Have I allowed "dry" times take me away from releasing the glory of God to others?

Ask the Holy Spirit:

- "Have I believed the lie that I am dry and far away from You?"
- "Come and fill me with a fresh awareness of Your refreshing waters."
- "Have I invited Your living waters to flow out of me towards others?"

Write in your journal what you hear Him say.

Day 23 DEVOTIONAL PRAYER

"Holy Spirit, I invite You to come and fill me once again to overflowing. I thank You that You've empowered me and filled me with Your living waters, and I pray that those waters will flow out of my life to be a demonstration of Your glory to those around me. Forgive me for believing the lie that You are far away and that I have nothing to give to others. Give me a greater awareness of what You've placed in my life, so that I can boldly release that glory to the world around me. Let the living waters in my life be used to bring You glory, and water the earth with the knowledge of Your goodness and splendor."

Declaration: I am becoming a river of God's glory, receiving His living water, and releasing it to others.

Journal

"The aim of spiritual formation is not behavior modification but the transformation of all those aspects of you and me where behavior comes from...Circumcision of the heart."
Dallas Willard

Day 24

REVELATION OF THE FRUIT OF THE HOLY SPIRIT

But the Holy Spirit produces this kind of fruit in our lives: love, joy, peace, patience, kindness, goodness, faithfulness, gentleness, and self-control. (Galatians 5:22-23, NLT)

OST OF THE TIME WHEN fruit comes up in discussion, we immediately think about the sweetness of an apple, or juiciness of an orange or peach, or perhaps the tartness of a lemon or lime. But the fact is, there are many fruits that we eat that never come to mind as being fruit, because they don't have the traditional characteristics we associate with fruit. For example, chili peppers, okra, tomatoes, zucchini, and eggplant are all fruits, but their tastes aren't sweet — so they feel more like vegetables.

Why are we talking about fruit? Because the way that we conduct our lives will always produce some kind of fruit; but the question is, what kind of fruit are we producing?

When Paul wrote his letter to the Galatians, he lists a number of qualities produced by a life lived in the Spirit. Having these present in our lives doesn't earn us right standing with God, but they are a good indicator of how much we're submitted to the Holy Spirit's work, because His work will always produce sweet-tasting fruit through us. Right before Paul lists the fruit of the Spirit, he pens another list of things produced through a life lived for selfishness: "sexual immorality, impurity, lustful pleasures, idolatry, sorcery, hostility, quarreling, jealousy, outbursts of anger, selfish ambition, dissension, division, envy, drunkenness, wild parties, and other sins like these." He then goes on to say that whoever is producing this bitter type of fruit will not inherit the Kingdom of God. Even if we produce some of the fruit of the Spirit in our lives, are we content with just a little, or are we allowing the Holy Spirit to work His character into our whole being? Do we still have some hold-outs and character deficiencies, or are we pressing in and giving access to God to all the places that need redeeming? Sure, we may not be going out and practicing sorcery or sleeping around, but is anger or jealousy still present? Do we allow pride and selfishness to stick around in our lives? You see, it's not about striving to not do what's wrong, but it's about setting our eyes on the giver of life, and inviting His work to be completed in us, so that His work is evident in our life's sweet tasting fruit.

Meditate on Galatians 5:22-23. Say it out loud a few times. Really think about how it applies to you. Ask yourself:

- What kind of fruit is evident in my life?
- Am I holding back and not allowing the Holy Spirit access to certain parts of my life?

Ask the Holy Spirit:

- "What areas of my life are not submitted to You?"
- "What kind of fruit are You producing in my life?"
- "What kind of fruit is selfishness producing in my life?"

Write in your journal what you hear Him say.

Day 24 DEVOTIONAL PRAYER

"Holy Spirit, I thank You for who You are. Thank You for always working in me. Thank You that You look after every part of my life. Thank You that You want to produce more of Your character in me. I invite Your continual, daily work, so that my life produces sweet-tasting fruit. Forgive me for holding on to certain places in my life and not submitting them to Your refinement. Forgive me for the bitter fruit that those poor choices have made. I ask that You would cleanse me and redeem those areas, so that the result of my life in You produces love, joy, peace, patience, kindness, goodness, faithfulness, gentleness, and self-control."

Declaration: My life is becoming a demonstration of the fruit of the Holy Spirit the more that I follow His lead.

Journal

"This experience, which Jesus spoke of as the new birth, is essential if we are to be transformed nonconformists ... Only through an inner spiritual transformation do we gain the strength to fight vigorously the evils of the world in a humble and loving spirit."
Martin Luther King, Jr.

Day 25

REVELATION OF THE FIRE OF THE HOLY SPIRIT

For our God is a consuming fire. (Hebrews 12:29, NLT)

OVER THE COURSE OF HUMAN HISTORY, fire has been an integral part of most families and communities. Fire provides warmth on a cold day, it provides the ability to cook food, and it provides light to see during the darkness of the evening. In the physical world, fire can be used when it's contained. However, left to itself, fire burns away anything in its path. If God is described as a consuming fire, we need to ask ourselves: what things in our lives are being burned off by His fire?

Fire is an important symbol in the Bible and it frequently represents purification, holiness, glory, and judgement. Because of the possible negative connotation of fire, believers can be hesitant about welcoming God's fire into their lives. It's true that the fire of the Holy Spirit most definitely refines us and purifies us, but what is often missing from the conversation is that you cannot separate the love of God from His fire. In fact, in the book of Revelation, we see the eyes of Jesus — His eyes of love — described as being as flames of fire. There is a big difference between being afraid of the Lord, and fearing the Lord. The fear of the Lord is a reverence motivated by love, which causes us to run towards Him. However, if we are afraid of God, it causes us to want to run away from Him. We all need to experience God's love, because that encounter will greatly affect how we choose to respond to His fire. There is no fear in God's love, for His perfect love casts out all fear. To the heart that loves God, the fire of the Holy Spirit is an empowering and consuming force, but to the heart that rejects God, a completely different type of encounter with His fire will occur. When we acknowledge His lordship and willingly lay our lives on the altar as a sacrifice of worship, God's fire comes and engulfs us in His love, His

111

essence, and His glory, transforming us into His image.

John the Baptist said that Jesus came not only to baptize us in the Holy Spirit, but also with fire (Luke 3:16). The fire of the Holy Spirit is the manifestation of God's very presence, His righteousness, His holiness, and His power. It is the baptism of the fire of Holy Spirit that works in us the desire for more of Christ's character, nature, and presence. Before the power of God can flow through us, the Holy Spirit's fire must first consume us. When we live in the fire of God, we become vessels of honor, purified and readied for the Master's use.

Meditate on Hebrews 12:29. Say it out loud a few times. Really think about how it applies to you. Ask yourself:

- Have I embraced the fire of the Holy Spirit in my life?
- Am I afraid of the fire of the Holy Spirit?

Ask the Holy Spirit:

- "Are there any lies that I am believing that are keeping me from embracing Your fire in my life?"
- "What does it look like for my life to be a living sacrifice of worship?"
- "How does Your fire enable Your power to flow through me?"

Write in your journal what you hear Him say.

Day 25 DEVOTIONAL PRAYER

"Holy Spirit, thank You for your presence. I set my gaze on You, Lord. I lay my life on the altar as a sacrifice of worship and a life lived unto You. Come, Holy Spirit, with Your fire. Purify, refine, and empower my heart with Your presence. Cause me to become ablaze with Your glory, and make me a living demonstration of Your power. Lord, burn in my heart a deep desire to know You more, to become more like You, and to be consumed by Your fire in every way."

Declaration: I am becoming a burning fire, consumed and purified by the holiness of God and blazing with the zeal of His love.

Journal

BECOMING FIRE

"Beware of harking back to what you once were when God wants you to be something you have never been."
Oswald Chambers

Day 26

REVELATION OF THE SEVEN SPIRITS OF GOD

And the Spirit of the Lord will rest on him — the Spirit of wisdom and understanding, the Spirit of counsel and might, the Spirit of knowledge and the fear of the Lord.
(Isaiah 11:2-3, NLT)

T HE HOLY SPIRIT IS NOT just a force or a spirit, but He is a person. As we begin to develop a relationship with the Holy Spirit, He comes and teaches, comforts, and empowers us to become like Christ Jesus.

When the prophet Isaiah described the Messiah in Isaiah 11, he spoke of the anointing of the Holy Spirit that will rest upon Him, and proceeds to give us seven aspects of the Holy Spirit that, examined together, provide a scope into His work in our lives:

The Spirit of the Lord — The Holy Spirit is the Lord. Just as the Father and Son are God, He is also God, equal in deity, power, and presence.

The Spirit of Wisdom — The Holy Spirit gives us the mind of God and teaches us God's ways.

The Spirit of Understanding — The Holy Spirit shows us how to apply the ways of God. He relates to us the realities of the heavenly and spiritual things of God.

The Spirit of Counsel — The Holy Spirit is the most excellent advisor. He reveals to us God's strategies and blueprints for establishing His Kingdom on the earth.

The Spirit of Might — The Holy Spirit empowers us to walk in the ways of God, to destroy the works of darkness, to become strong and bold in the Lord, and to overcome every obstacle in our path.

The Spirit of Knowledge — The Holy Spirit searches the deep things of God and reveals to us things that we did not know before. He teaches about the Father and Jesus, imparting to us supernatural knowledge, leading us into an experiential knowledge of God, not just an informational knowing.

The Spirit of the Fear of the Lord — The Holy Spirit reveals to us the majesty and the supremacy of Jesus. He brings us into a revelation of the greatness of the Father, leading us to love, respect, honor, and revere the Lord as the source of all things. This is what keeps us on the path of righteousness and in pursuit of God's heart.

The Holy Spirit is such a wonderful gift to us, and He wants to fill us and rest upon us so that we walk in the same anointing on the earth that Jesus had. WOW!

Meditate on Isaiah 11:2-3. Say it out loud a few times. Really think about how it applies to you. Ask yourself:
- Have I considered the different aspects of the Holy Spirit?
- What aspects of the Holy Spirit do I have yet to encounter?

Ask the Holy Spirit:
- "Holy Spirit, have I related to You as a force or as a person?"
- "Holy Spirit, will You reveal yourself to me in every aspect listed in these verses?"
- "Holy Spirit, am I harboring any unbelief that is keeping me from knowing You in all these aspects?

Write in your journal what you hear Him say.

Day 26 DEVOTIONAL PRAYER

"Holy Spirit, I am in awe of who You are. I invite You to come and fill my whole being. Thank You for inviting me into a relationship with You. I repent of not relating to You as a person and ask You to reveal Yourself to me in a tangible way. I submit to Your leading and Your Lordship. Lead me on the paths of righteousness and in the ways of God. Thank You for revealing to me the Father and Son. Let the power of Your presence make me a demonstration to those around me of Your love, goodness, and glory."

Declaration: I am becoming more aware of the person of the Holy Spirit and allowing all of His characteristics to bring change in my life.

Journal

"Transformation is not a formula, it is obedience to the nudging of the Holy Spirit who is the agent of transformation."
Mark J. Chironna

Day 27

REVELATION OF THE ANOINTING OF THE HOLY SPIRIT

"The Spirit of the Lord is upon Me, because He has anointed Me to preach the gospel to the poor; He has sent Me to heal the broken-hearted, to proclaim liberty to the captives and recovery of sight to the blind, to set at liberty those who are oppressed; to proclaim the acceptable year of the Lord." (Luke 4:18-19, NKJV)

THE WORLD IS IN BONDAGE. People are weighed down by the sins that they carry, and are slaves to the spirit of fear and death that they've come into agreement with. Even though many feel that they are free, the reality is that a yoke of slavery has been placed on the neck of every person on this planet, and the only way to be freed from this burden is through Christ and the anointing of the Holy Spirit.

The passage above is about the story of Jesus reading Scriptures out loud in the synagogue in Nazareth, where He quoted a prophecy of Isaiah which had been penned around 700 years earlier. After Jesus finished reading, He sat down and said, "Today this Scripture is fulfilled." We don't have to imagine what the religious people thought of this statement, because Scripture records that they were filled with wrath at the perceived audacious words of Jesus, so much so that they tried to throw Him off a cliff to kill Him.

Throughout His life, Jesus taught and equipped His followers to become like Him, and to continue the work that He started. We are called to walk in the same anointing that Jesus carried 2,000 years ago, which was used to break off the chains of the enemy. 1 John 2 says that "you have an anointing from the Holy One," so we can confidently believe that the Holy Spirit has empowered us to walk with Him, for the purpose of crushing the enemy's works. Isaiah 10 tells us it is the anointing that breaks the yoke. This means that the fulfillment of Luke 4 in our lives will not be accomplished through our polished speech, good singing voices, skills, or good works, but through the Holy Spirit's anointing that rests on us. Unfortunately, the professionalism of Christianity has led to valuing gifting over anointing. Well-spoken pastors are often able to use their gifting to gather lots of people into their churches, but without anointing, that gifting will only go so far — and it often leaves the people in a state of immaturity.

It's truly the anointing of the Holy Spirit that will help usher in freedom and break off the yoke of slavery that has this world bound. God's mercies are new every morning, so let's press in for greater levels of empowerment, and not be content with yesterday's anointing.

Meditate on Luke 4:18-19. Say it out loud a few times. Really think about how it applies to you. Ask yourself:
  • Have I even considered whether I'm anointed or not?
  • Do I believe that God's anointing can use my life to bring freedom to others?

Ask the Holy Spirit:
  • "Have I asked You for Your anointing?"
  • "Do I trust more in my gifting than I do in my anointing?"
  • "Am I intentional about using the anointing You've given me to see freedom come to those around me?"

Write in your journal what you hear Him say.

Day 27 DEVOTIONAL PRAYER

"Holy Spirit, You empower those who draw close to You. You anoint those who seek Your Kingdom. I ask You to fill me once again to overflowing. Fill me with Your presence, and fill me with Your peace. I ask You to anoint my life, so that I can be effective in breaking off the yoke of bondage that the enemy has on those around me. Use my life, words, and actions in a powerful way that brings healing and restoration to the broken places. Forgive me for relying on my gifts instead of on Your anointing. Let me walk in confidence, knowing that You have empowered my life to bring Your freedom, and to see Your Kingdom come in a greater way."

Declaration: I am becoming one who breaks off the chains of the enemy and extends God's Kingdom through His anointing on me.

Journal

"When we accept Christ, however, there should be a transformation, a complete change from selfish people to selfless people."
Mark J. Musser

REVELATION OF THE GIFTS OF THE HOLY SPIRIT

Pursue love, yet earnestly desire spiritual gifts......
(1 Corinthians 14:1a, NASB)

LL CHILDREN LOVE TO RECEIVE GIFTS. Some of our best memories from childhood involved celebrations where our parents and friends gave us gifts. As children of God, there are special gifts that the Father, Son, and the Holy Spirit have determined to give to us. The Holy Spirit's gifts are gifts that empower and equip us to demonstrate Jesus Christ to the world around us.

Just like gifts we receive in the natural, the spiritual gifts of the Holy Spirit come in many varieties, with many effects and different types of manifestations. He has given each of us unique mixes of these gifts. 1 Corinthians 12 tells us about the specific gifts He has given: "But to each one is given the manifestation of the Spirit for the common good. For to one is given the word of wisdom through the Spirit, and to another the word of knowledge according to the same Spirit; to another faith by the same Spirit, and to another gifts of healing by the one Spirit, and to another the effecting of miracles, and to another prophecy and to another the distinguishing of spirits, to another various kinds of tongues, and to another the interpretation of tongues. But one and the same Spirit works all these things, distributing to each one individually just as He wills." All these gifts are available to us through the Holy Spirit. But we must realize that we cannot earn spiritual gifts, because they are gifts and not awards. Just like you can't earn God's love, you can't earn gifts—you are given them; but this also means that we can ask for the ones that we don't have. The principle of asking is a key principle in the New Testament. "Ask and it will be given to you, seek and you will find, knock and the door will be opened to you." (Matt 7:7).

One thing we must guard against is focusing too much on what is being given, and losing sight of the Giver. After Paul lists these gifts, in the next chapter he exhorts us to first pursue love. We know that love is a person, because the Bible says that God is love. God's love must be the vehicle for the demonstration of our gifts. If love isn't present, then God isn't present, and what we are releasing to others will be from ourselves and not from Him. So let's be diligent to pursue Love Himself, and show ourselves to be much loved children of God. Let us ask Him boldly to reveal and empower us with His gifts, so that we will demonstrate the Kingdom of God and God's love to the world around us.

Meditate on 1 Corinthians 14:1. Say it out loud a few times. Really think about how it applies to you. Ask yourself:

- Have I considered that I have been given spiritual gifts by the Holy Spirit?
- Do I understand why the Holy Spirit has given me gifts?

Ask the Holy Spirit:

- "What gifts have you already placed inside of me?"
- "Am I focused on pursuing Your gifts or am I truly pursuing You?"
- "Am I intentional about using the gifts you have given me to lead people to Christ, or to myself?

Write in your journal what you hear Him say.

Day 28 DEVOTIONAL PRAYER

"Holy Spirit, thank You for loving me and giving me gifts that will enable me to become more like Jesus, and demonstrate His love to others. Give me a heart that wants to know You above all things, even Your gifts. Holy Spirit, illuminate my heart with a fresh understanding of the Father's love. Let me not find my affirmation from the gifts I have, but from Your love. Let Your love flow through me so that the gifts You have given me would operate in power, leading others to Your heart. Holy Spirit, I ask for more faith, and for You to enlarge my capacity to trust You and to believe that when I ask You for Your gifts, You will be faithful to give them to me. In Jesus's name."

Declaration: My life is becoming a powerful demonstration of the love of God by allowing the gifts of the Holy Spirit to flow out of me to others.

"If we understand that everything happening to us is to make us more Christlike, it will solve a great deal of anxiety in our lives."
A. W. Tozer

Day 29

REVELATION OF THE COMMISSIONS OF JESUS

"Go into all the world and preach the gospel to all creation, make disciples of all nations, baptizing them in the name of the Father and of the Son and of the Holy Spirit, (and) if you forgive anyone's sins, they are forgiven. If you do not forgive them, they are not forgiven. Stay...until you have been clothed with power from on high (and) baptized with the Holy Spirit." (Mark 16:15, Matthew 6:10, John 20:23, Luke 24:49, Acts 1:5)

IT'S EASY TO LOOK AT the chaos that's all over the world and be cynical about the future. The media is all about garnering as much attention as possible, so the more negative stories they push, the more "eyeballs" they get to watch. Because of this, it's pretty obvious that they're not in the news business anymore, but in the business of selling fear. Unfortunately, many in the church have fallen into the trap of listening to bad news, instead of spreading the good news. They are being discipled more by culture than they are being empowered by the Holy Spirit.

A large portion of the church has checked itself out of being a relevant force of good, because they've bought into the lie that the purpose of life looks like holding on until Jesus comes back. Their dominant thought is "What's the point in trying to make this world a better place if everything is going to continually grow darker anyway?" This has caused many Christians to take themselves out of their purpose of extending God's Kingdom in favor of holding on to their own little kingdoms. Does this really sound like the actions of a victorious people? Does this really line up with what Jesus commissioned the church to do?

Jesus told us to forgive sins, to heal the sick, to cast out demons, to bring people to salvation, and to disciple nations. He told us that we would accomplish these things through the empowerment and baptism of the Holy Spirit. God has chosen to partner with His children to see all of these things accomplished, and His invitation is the same as it was 2,000 years ago: "Be My hands and feet to the world." Often we ask God to be the answer for what ails our cities and nations, when He is saying, "I've commissioned and anointed you to be the answer." A powerful church daily commits itself to walk in confidence, knowing that Jesus has called us, commissioned us, and anointed us to walk in His power and authority, and to see His Kingdom come in a greater way.

Meditate on the passages listed. Say them out loud a few times. Really think about how it applies to you. Ask yourself:

- Do I view the commissions of Jesus as a personal invitation for me to accomplish?
- Do I believe that the Holy Spirit has anointed me?

Ask the Holy Spirit:

- "Have I invited Your baptism and empowerment to fall upon me?"
- "Have I been intentional about fulfilling the commissions of Jesus?"
- "Do I have the faith to believe that You will use me to heal the sick and cast out demons?"

Write in your journal what you hear Him say.

Day 29 DEVOTIONAL PRAYER

"God, I believe that You've called me to be Your hands and feet to a dying world. You've commissioned me to walk in power and authority and to represent Your Kingdom, which is righteousness and peace and joy in the Holy Spirit. Forgive me for being afraid and not fulfilling the commissions of Jesus. Today, I choose to walk in confidence, knowing that You've empowered me to bring salvation, healing, and deliverance to those around me. I choose to not give my ears to the negative reports of this world, but instead I choose to declare the good news of the Kingdom."

Declaration: I am becoming one who obeys the commissions of Jesus to bring salvation, healing, and deliverance to those around me.

"The Bible was not given for our information but for our transformation."
Dwight L. Moody

REVELATION OF THE ECCLESIA

"Your kingdom come, Your will be done, on earth as it is in heaven."
(Matthew 6:10, ESV)

JESUS WOULDN'T HAVE GIVEN US a prayer to pray, if He didn't intend for it to be answered. When He taught His disciples to pray "on earth as it is in heaven," He wasn't just including some cute words about a nice idea, but He was commissioning us, and telling us that this is what we are to believe and contend for. Jesus is coming back to a victorious church without spot or wrinkle, not some weak, cowering, self-focused group of people who want to leave the planet as soon as possible. Revelation 11 speaks of the earth in the last days this way: "The kingdom of the world has become the kingdom of our Lord and of His Christ, and He shall reign forever and ever." Yes, there's darkness around us, but that's precisely why Jesus commissioned His *ecclesia* (the Greek word for church) to become a powerful force to help usher His glory and light into the places that the enemy has hijacked. The first time the gospels record Jesus using the word "church," He said that He was giving His bride the keys to His Kingdom, and commissioned us to bind and loose things on earth that we see being bound and loosed in heaven. This doesn't sound like a weak and defeated group of people, but rather agents of change who partner with heaven to bring healing to a world that is in desperate need of salvation.

The Greek word *ecclesia* literally means "a called-out assembly" and it was used to describe a political gathering. Over the last two millennia, much of the church has taken this literal translation to heart, as it has removed itself from society and quietly conducted its spiritual business, while leaving the world to its own devices. But was this what Jesus really meant when He first spoke of His church? At the time He used this term, Israel was under Roman rule. The Romans adopted that word, and used it to describe a group of people who were commissioned by Caesar to go into conquered nations and make those nations become like Rome. The *ecclesia*, led by an *apostle*, would infiltrate every mountain of society, and began discipling them in the ways of Rome. Their goal was to get those conquered nations to begin thinking like Rome, so they would eventually integrate into Roman ways and never rise up in resistance. This is the word and the context that Jesus used to describe what He wanted the church to become, but instead of spreading the message of Rome, He called His people to spread the gospel of His Kingdom. His bride was never intended to be a quiet, irrelevant group who kept to themselves, but a group of laid-down lovers of Christ, who seek first His Kingdom, and walk in the fire and power of the Holy Spirit to see His Kingdom come to earth, just as it is in heaven.

Meditate on Matthew 6:10. Say it out loud a few times. Really think about how it applies to you. Ask yourself:

- What does it look like for God's will to be done on earth?
- Do I believe God can use me to bring His Kingdom to the earth?

Ask the Holy Spirit:

- "Have I been content in sitting on the sidelines?"
- "Have I checked out of my purpose and calling to extend Your Kingdom?"
- "Do I believe that You have empowered me to demonstrate Your Kingdom on the earth?"

Write in your journal what you hear Him say.

Day 30 DEVOTIONAL PRAYER

"God, I thank You that You have chosen to partner with me to see Your Kingdom come to the Earth. I am a part of the bride of Christ, and we have been called to infiltrate every corner of the world that the enemy has stolen, and bring the glory of God to those places. Forgive me for believing the lie that I am insignificant, and for focusing on building my own kingdom. I choose to seek Your Kingdom first, and I believe that through my words and actions Your Kingdom will be extended. Let my battle cry be, 'On Earth as it is in Heaven!'"

Declaration: I am a part of the church that is becoming who it is called to be: a transformational force of influence and change to a dying world.

Journal

"Therefore, if anyone is in Christ, he is a new creation. The old has passed away; behold, the new has come."
The Apostle Paul

ABOUT THE AUTHORS

Ty and Daneen Bottler are speakers, equippers, worship leaders, and authors based out
of Portland, Oregon. They carry a message of
transformation through encountering God's
presence. Both Ty and Daneen walk in an ap-
ostolic / prophetic anointing that brings people, churches and regions into alignment with
the heart of the Father, by understanding their
true identity.
Ty and Daneen have been married for over twenty-five years and
have two wonderful children, Trenton & Kylie. They serve as the exec-
utive pastors of Father's House City Ministries, a church in downtown
Portland, Oregon, where they champion the message of city transformation. They have had the honor of speaking, leading worship, and
consulting in a number of churches and conferences throughout the
United States and Canada, as well as equipping many in the body of
Christ through various books and schools.
For additional resources, including books and music by Ty
and Daneen, or to find out more about the authors, please visit:
www.tyanddaneenbottler.com